THE
WIT AND WISDOM
OF
TED KENNEDY

THE
WIT AND WISDOM
OF
TED KENNEDY

*A Treasury of Reflections, Statements of Belief,
and Calls to Action*

EDITED BY BILL ADLER & BILL ADLER, JR.

PEGASUS BOOKS
NEW YORK

THE WIT AND WISDOM OF TED KENNEDY

Pegasus Books LLC
80 Broad Street, 5th Floor
New York, NY 10004

Collection copyright © 2009 by Bill Adler and Bill Adler, Jr.

First Pegasus Books edition November 2009

Interior design by Maria Fernandez

Library of Congress Cataloging-in-Publication Data is available.

ISBN: 978-1-60598-112-3

10 9 8 7 6 5 4 3 2 1

Printed in the United States of America
Distributed by W. W. Norton & Company

For my father (and co-editor), who created the
Wit and Wisdom book idea, and who showed me
how much fun the publishing world is.

—Bill Adler, Jr.

CONTENTS

---- ∞∞∞ ----

INTRODUCTION

Individual faults and frailties are no excuse to give in—and no exemption from the common obligation to give of ourselves.

—Ted Kennedy

Senator Edward Kennedy was one of the most influential and important leaders of our generation, and will be remembered as one of the most significant politicians in the history of the United States.

Ted Kennedy was the son of Ambassador Joseph Kennedy, brother of Attorney General Robert Kennedy and brother of President John Fitzgerald Kennedy: It can be said that in his lifetime Ted Kennedy accomplished more than any of them to better America.

Kennedy was elected to the United States Senate nine times and when he died he was the third longest serving Senator in United States history. When elected to the United States Senate in 1962, he was just 30 years old—the minimum age to serve.

Ted Kennedy was a champion of civil rights, health care, the war on AIDS, gun control, education, drug benefits for seniors, and myriad other issues that affect Americans every day. Kennedy stood his ground on these issues, unwavering in his convictions, despite the political vicissitudes of the years. Though known as a stalwart of the Democratic party, he was always able to work with his Republican colleagues as well as Republican presidents to achieve his dreams. Paying fond tribute to him at his funeral mass were two of his oldest friends in the Senate, Republicans John McCain and Orrin Hatch.

In 1964, I (Bill Adler, Sr.) edited *The Kennedy Wit*, a tribute to President John F. Kennedy published soon after his assassination. That book was an international bestseller because the slain president occupied a special and unique place in the hearts of Americans. Robert Kennedy's death followed less than five years later. Ted Kennedy became the Kennedy brother to whom we looked for hope and inspiration. Over his long time of service in the Senate, he developed into a leader of vision and unwavering perseverance. He, like his brothers John and Robert, looked ahead and all saw how we could make America a better place.

When I compiled *The Kennedy Wit* I was 32 years old. I'm 80 now. A lot has changed over the decades, and much of the change that has bettered our nation can be attributed to the hard work and vision of Ted Kennedy. I'm grateful for that.

President Barack Obama said this of Ted Kennedy at his memorial service on August 29, 2009:

> "Today we say goodbye to the youngest child of Rose and Joseph Kennedy. The world will long remember their son Edward as the heir to a weighty legacy; a champion for those who had none; the soul of the Democratic Party; and the lion of the U.S. Senate—a man whose name graces nearly one thousand laws, and who penned more than three hundred himself.
>
> "We can still hear his voice bellowing through the Senate chamber, face reddened, fist pounding the podium, a veritable force of nature, in support of health care or workers' rights or civil rights. And yet, while his causes became deeply personal, his disagreements never did. While he was seen by his fiercest

critics as a partisan lightning rod, that is not the prism through which Ted Kennedy saw the world, nor was it the prism through which his colleagues saw him. He was a product of an age when the joy and nobility of politics prevented differences of party and philosophy from becoming barriers to cooperation and mutual respect—a time when adversaries still saw each other as patriots."

Senator Kennedy's life was deepened by tragedy and strengthened by a joyous love of humanity. And it was perhaps this sad and wonderful combination of influences that made him care more for ordinary Americans than most other politicians. After he lost his bid for the presidency he devoted his life to becoming a great Senator.

Through Ted Kennedy's wit and wisdom we can understand and appreciate this great man. And perhaps become better Americans ourselves.

THE
WIT AND WISDOM
OF
TED KENNEDY

WORDS OF INSPIRATION

THE KENNEDY NAME HAS LONG BEEN ASSOCIATED WITH soaring words and inspirational utterances. When we think of President John F. Kennedy, we can hear his ringing call to serve: "Ask not what your country can do for you; ask what you can do for your country." When we think of Bobby Kennedy, we may remember him best by his bold vision for a better future: "Some men see things as they are, and say 'Why?'—I dream of things that never were, and say, 'Why not?'"

These two lives were cut tragically short, but even so, they left words that will continue to inspire Americans for generations to come. We are more fortunate when it comes to the life of their youngest brother, Senator Edward M. Kennedy, who was granted 77 years to make a difference with his life.

The third-longest serving senator in U.S. history has had 46 years to address us in speeches, statements, and other prepared remarks, as well as informal comments and recorded conversations. When in front of a large crowd he was often a rousing orator, a stem-winder, but not all the quotations in this chapter were delivered in a booming voice from a podium; there are some that come across equally well—perhaps better—when the reader is alone in a quiet room.

It was always a pleasure to search for and find these nuggets. We listened to many hours of videotapes of speeches, read through essays, and combed through public statements, and so often found ourselves stopping to appreciate some felicitous phrase, some lilting combination of words that reminded us that he was more than a moving speaker: He was truly a fine wordsmith. Of course, we know that Senator Kennedy also employed some supremely talented speechwriters, but in the end—as some of those speechwriters have noted in interviews about the experience of working with him—the choice of words was always his.

When it came to the music of the English language to move us to the heights, Senator Kennedy had perfect pitch.

The work goes on, the cause endures, the hope still lives and the dream shall never die.

—Democratic National Convention,
August 12, 1980

Let each of us, to the best of our ability, in our own day and generation, perform something worthy to be remembered. . . . Let us give something back to America, in return for all it has given us.

—Speech, March 1, 1976

I have seen throughout my life how we as a people can rise to a challenge, embrace change and renew our destiny.

—Speech at Harvard, December 2008

If I can leave a single message with the younger generation, it is to lash yourself to the mast, like Ulysses, if you want to escape the siren calls of complacency and indifference.

—Speech, June 4, 1978

Yes, we are all Americans. This is what we do. We reach the moon. We scale the heights. I know it. I've seen it. I've lived it. And we can do it again.

—*Democratic National Convention,*
August 12, 2008

The commitment I seek is not to outworn views but to old values that will never wear out. Programs may sometimes become obsolete, but the ideal of fairness always endures. Circumstances may change, but the work of compassion must continue.

—*Democratic National Convention,*
August 12, 1980

It is true, as has been said on this floor, that prejudice exists in the minds and hearts of men. It cannot be eradicated by law. But I firmly believe a sense of fairness and good will also exists in the minds and hearts of men side by side with the prejudice; a sense of fairness and good will which shows itself so often in acts of charity and kindness toward others. This noble characteristic wants to come out. It wants to, and often does, win out against the prejudice. Law, expressing as it does the moral conscience of the community, can help it come out in every person, so in the end the prejudice will be dissolved.

—from Kennedy's first speech on the Senate floor, April, 9, 1964

Our progressive vision is not just for Democrats or Republicans, for red states or blue states. It's a way forward for the nation as a whole—to a new prosperity and greater opportunity for all—a vision not just of the country we can become, but of the country we must become—an America that embraces the values and aspirations of our people now, and for coming generations.

—Address at the National Press Club, Washington, DC, January 12, 2005

We must insist that our children and our grand-children shall inherit a land which they can truly call America the beautiful.

—Democratic National Convention, August 12, 1980

It is our moral duty . . . to ensure our security but also to reflect our humanity. That is our calling. We should keep out those who would harm us, but welcome those who will contribute to America. We must protect our communities and our nation with laws that are just and fair. But we must also provide a path for honest, hardworking people to emerge from the shadows and earn the privilege of American citizenship.

—National Hispanic Prayer Breakfast,
June 8, 2006

Since I was a boy, I have known the joy of sailing the waters off Cape Cod. And for all my years in public life, I have believed that America must sail toward the shores of liberty and justice for all. There is no end to that journey, only the next great voyage. We know the future will outlast all of us, but I believe that all of us will live on in the future we make.

—Speech at Harvard, December 2008

A new American majority is ready to respond to our call for a revitalized American dream—grounded firmly in our Constitution and in the endless adventure of lifting this nation to ever new heights of discovery, prosperity, progress, and service to all people and to all humanity.

—Address to the National Press Club,
Washington, DC,
January 12, 2005

Traveling across the length and breadth of America, taking the measure of our people, you cannot help but come away with a sense that we can do the job—that our problems are only human, and the solutions will be human, too; that America is a land whose people have the capacity to solve its problems many times over, if only we let them try.

—Speech to the National Jaycees Convention,
Portland, OR, June 15, 1971

More than four decades ago, near this place [the Lincoln Memorial], Martin Luther King called on the nation to let freedom ring. Freedom did ring—and freedom can ring again. It is time for Americans to lift their voices now—in pride for our immigrant past and in pride for our immigrant future.

> —*"I Stand With You" Speech*
> *at Immigration Rally,*
> *April 10, 2006*

Don't sacrifice your political convictions for the convenience of the hour.

> —*As quoted by William Safire in his 1990 book,*
> Words of Wisdom: More Good Advice

There are some who seek to wreck the peace process. They are blinded by fear of a future they cannot imagine—a future in which respect for differences is a healing and unifying force. They are driven by an anger that holds no respect for life—even for the lives of children. But a new spirit of hope is gaining momentum. It can banish the fear that blinds. It can conquer the anger that fuels the merchants of violence. We are building an irresistible force that can make the immovable object move.

—University of Ulster, Derry, Northern Ireland, January 9, 1988

I love the flag no less because I believe that America has lost its way in Vietnam. I love the flag no less because I want America to move ahead and right the wrongs we see in our society at home. Those of us who push America on do so out of love and hope for the America that can be.

—Fourth of July address, Wakefield, MA, 1970

[We] are . . . good neighbors. The settlers traveled to the West in wagon trains because they knew that the survival of their families depended on strong communities working together for the common good. They lived by the Golden Rule not only as a moral mandate, but as a necessity. That is our American heritage. Neighbor helping neighbor. All of us contributing to our communities and to our nation to make them stronger.

—Speech, March 14, 2005

No nation is guaranteed a position of lasting prosperity and security. We have to work for it. We have to fight for it. We have to sacrifice for it. We have a choice. We can continue to be buffeted by the harsh winds of a shrinking world. Or we can think anew, and guide the currents of globalization with a new progressive vision that strengthens America and equips our citizens to move confidently to the future.

—*Address at the National Press Club,*
Washington, DC, January 12, 2005

The Bible gives us an excellent ancient example of power, justice and love coming together in the course of human events. That example is God's work on behalf of the Israelites while they were in bondage, during 40 years of wandering in the wilderness, and in the midst of their many battles for independence. This same God inspired Dr. [Martin Luther] King to boldly proclaim the vision of a new America, undivided by race, religion, or gender—an America where the ingenuity, creativity and industry of African-Americans is welcomed—an America built on the principles of one nation under God, indivisible, with liberty and justice for all.

—Remarks on Martin Luther King, Jr. Holiday, Peoples Congregational United Church of Christ, January 14, 2001

This November the torch will be passed again to a new generation of Americans, so with Barack Obama and for you and for me, our country will be committed to his cause. The work begins anew. The hope rises again. And the dream lives on.

—Speech at the Democratic National Convention, August 25, 2008

ON DEFINING MOMENTS IN
OUR HISTORY

EARLY ON IN OUR TASK OF CATALOGUING SENATOR Kennedy's writings and speeches, we began to see a clear and consistent pattern emerge: each was imbued with a deep appreciation of history. For every event he has commemorated, for every policy advocated or opposed, he notes much more than its impact on our present lives but takes care to measure its place in the tapestry of our times, its ties to the past and its significance for our future.

We see this in his congratulatory remarks upon the election of the first African-American president, Barack Obama, as well as in his somber reflections on the day after the 9/11 terrorist attacks. It's there, too, in his measured words of resistance to the Bush Administration's drumbeat toward war in Iraq.

Far more often than the standard politician, Senator Kennedy draws upon the wisdom of past leaders and the lessons of the historical record to present his understanding of a challenge or crisis in the here-and-now. We did a quick experiment to prove the point, choosing twenty speeches and policy statements at random, and found not a single one lacking a reference to the roots of the issue under consideration or a citation of the work of a historian of the subject, or the insight of a leader who had dealt with the issue before. In a few cases, the citation was to something said by his brother Jack or Bobby, for it is clear that Ted Kennedy's appreciation for the role of history is due in no small measure to having grown up in a family whose children were imbued from their earliest years with a sense of our history and their places in it.

With Barack Obama we will close the book on the old politics of race against race, gender against gender, ethnic group against ethnic group, and straight against gay.
—*Endorsement of Senator Barack Obama*
for president, American University,
January 2008

Yesterday's [September 11] terrorist atrocities against innocent Americans were vicious and horrifying. They were acts of unspeakable cruelty unleashed against the American people in a shameful attempt to spread chaos throughout our nation and instill fear in the hearts of our citizens. But such acts will not succeed, and they never will succeed.

No American will ever forget watching a hijacked civilian aircraft crash into the towers of the World Trade Center, or seeing the plume of smoke rise from the Pentagon in the aftermath of the terrorist attack. No American will ever forget the sense of anger and vulnerability that swept our nation yesterday, when thousands of innocent lives were suddenly and senselessly ended by these vicious acts.

My heart goes out to the victims of this attack and their loved ones. The American people share our anger, our grief—and our resolve. We cannot bring back the lives of the fathers, mothers, sons, daughters, brothers, sisters, relatives, and friends—although we wish desperately that we could. We cannot yet fully answer the complex questions that haunt the country about this atrocity. As we search for and find the answers, we pray for the victims and their loved ones, and we hope that they will find a measure of peace and comfort from our prayers.

This is a massive tragedy for America, and we must make clear that our national resolve will not be weakened. Our country has been tested and tried in the past, and we have always emerged stronger and wiser. We will do so again now. America's commitment to the values of freedom and justice.

—Statement on the Terrorist Attacks
in New York and Washington, DC,
September 12, 2001

History will now say on this impeachment, as they said on the impeachment of Andrew Johnson, that it was the radical Republicans. . . . And that is going to be the judgment of history.

—Speech opposing the impeachment
of President Bill Clinton

We are now at a major cross-road in our history. The 9/11 atrocities have forced us all to think profoundly about what is great in America. All through our shock and grief, the people's courage never failed. 9/11 was one of the nation's saddest hours, but the response was one of our finest hours.

That hour must not be lost. It can mark the beginning of a new era of common purpose—a return to policies which truly reflect America's values, a return to the genuine pursuit of justice. The unselfishness we saw in 2001 must not give way to selfishness in 2003. The noble caring for one another that we celebrated then must not be succeeded now by a retreat from our ideals.

Yes, our country is strong. But it can be stronger—not just in the power we hold, but in the promise we fulfill of a nation that truly does make better the life of the world. If we rededicate ourselves to that great goal, our achievements will reverberate around the globe, and America will be admired anew for what it must be now, in this new time, more than ever—"the last, best hope of earth."

—Statement on American values and
war with Iraq, March 13, 2003

I am announcing today my candidacy for the Senate of the United States. I make this decision in full knowledge of the obstacles I will face, the charges that will be made, and the heavy responsibilities of the office to which I aspire. . . . The Senate is surely one of the most important bodies in the Free World. Each year its decisions affect the hopes and lives of men and women in every part of the globe, in every state of the Union and in every town, city, and county in Massachusetts. In the months and years immediately ahead, the Senate will be deciding whether our younger citizens will receive the education they need—whether our older citizens will receive the medical care they need—whether our transportation system will flourish or falter—whether our cities will obtain new industries and whether our industries will obtain new contracts and new markets at home and abroad—whether our tax laws, our immigration laws, our anti-recession safeguards and our anti-crime laws are to be modernized and made more effective.

—Announcing his candidacy for
United States Senate,
March 14, 1962

This disaster reminds us that we are all part of the American family and we have a responsibility to help members of that family when they are in need.

*—Speaking of Hurricane Katrina
at the presentation of the 2005
Robert F. Kennedy Human Rights Award
to Stephen Bradberry of New Orleans,
November, 2005*

Historians of the future will wonder about the years we have just passed through. They will ask how it could be, a century after the Civil War, that black and white had not learned to live together in the promise of this land.

—Speech, January 26, 1976

When missiles were discovered in Cuba—missiles more threatening to us than anything Saddam [Hussein] has today—some in the highest councils of government urged an immediate and unilateral strike. Instead the United States took its case to the United Nations, won the endorsement of the Organization of

American States, and brought along even our most skeptical allies. We imposed a blockade, demanded inspection, and insisted on the removal of the missiles.

When an earlier President outlined that choice to the American people and the world, he spoke of it in realistic terms—not with a sense that the first step would necessarily be the final step, but with a resolve that it must be tried.

As he said then, "Action is required . . . and these actions [now] may only be the beginning. We will not prematurely or unnecessarily risk the costs of . . . war—but neither will we shrink from that risk at any time it must be faced."

In 2002, we too can and must be both resolute and measured. In that way, the United States prevailed without war in the greatest confrontation of the Cold War. Now, on Iraq, let us build international support, try the United Nations, and pursue disarmament before we turn to armed conflict.

—Remarks about the prospect of a
U.S. invasion of Iraq,
September 27, 2002

We face no more serious decision in our democracy than whether or not to go to war.

—Comment on the Bush Doctrine
of Pre-emptive War,
October 7, 2002

Just as the 20th Century was the century of the physical sciences, the 21st Century will be the century of the life sciences. In the last century, we developed the automobile, the computer, and the rocket ship. We unlocked the secrets of the smallest atomic particles and peered into the vastness of space.

This new century is still young, but it has already witnessed astonishing breakthroughs in medical research. Scientists have mapped the human genome—a task that once seemed inconceivable. Cracking the code of life will have profound implications for the treatment and prevention of disease. Treatments can be prescribed based on an individual's genetic signature to prevent side effects. Diseases can be diagnosed and treated before symptoms appear.

—Speech at the Kennedy Library,
April 28, 2002

Our struggle is not with some monarch named George who inherited the crown—although it often seems that way.

—*Comment about President George W. Bush*

Every society is a mixture of stability and change, an irrevocable history and an uncertain future. We are both what we have been and what we desire to be. We are creatures of memory and hope, struggling with uncertainty as we try to fulfill the promises we know we must keep. Thus our society is in constant flux—different today from what it was yesterday—a continuation of the past, part of an organic process with roots deep in the history of our nations and of our common ancestors. Societies are like rivers, flowing from fixed and ancient sources through channels cut over the centuries—yet no man can ever step in the same water in which he stood only a moment ago.

—*Address at the Bicentennial of Trinity College,*
Dublin, Ireland,
March 3, 1970

It is not by accident that America over the years has been able to combine the wisdom of Athens and the might of Sparta. We have been a nation thrice blessed: blessed once with abundant natural resources; blessed a second time with a resourceful and stubborn citizenry; blessed a third time with a system of self-government that has reconciled, perhaps more perfectly than any other nation in history, the aspirations of individual freedom with the requirements of social order.

—Speech, April 30, 1979

One by one, issue by issue, program by program, the Republican Right has methodically turned away from policies which brought about a century of progress for working Americans. They want to build the 21st century economy on 19th century economic values, as if the last 100 years had not occurred. For them, the law of the jungle is the best economic policy for America—not equal opportunity, not fairness, not the American dream. Their policies will inevitably result in a lesser America, and have already meant a growing gulf between rich and poor.

—Speech, "Creating a Genuine 'Opportunity Society,'" March 1, 2004

More than any of our Presidents, John Adams secured the institutions of the freedoms and the democracy that we have enjoyed for many generations of Americans. John Adams helped bind an emerging young nation by appointing George Washington, a southerner, to lead the largely northern Continental Army—one of the first acts of national unity. . . . John Adams laid the basis for our independent judiciary by appointing John Marshall to the Supreme Court. From his influence on the Constitution, his belief in the importance of a bicameral legislature, his insistence on a separation of powers and an independent judiciary—to his service as the nation's first Vice-President and second President—Adams' marks on our political institutions and judicial system are unique in our nation's history.

—Statement Proposing a National Memorial
in Honor of President John Adams,
April 5, 2001

The fall of the Ottoman Empire at the beginning of this century is widely attributed to the excesses of a top-heavy civil service and a system of administrative regulation imposed by a bureaucracy run wild. The traditional American reaction to a problem or abuse has been to say, "There ought to be a law." But now, as we survey the complex legal framework of the nation, we should also be prepared to say of many areas, "There ought *not* to be a law."

—*Speech, June 14, 1979*

It is time for all governments, political leaders and peoples everywhere to recognize the Armenian Genocide. These annual commemorations are an effective way to pay tribute to the courage and suffering and triumph of the Armenian people, and to ensure that such atrocities will never happen again to any people on earth.

—*Statement on the 86th Anniversary*
of the Armenian Genocide,
April 4, 2001

Even without the bonds of blood and history, the deepening tragedy of Ulster today would demand that voices of concerned Americans everywhere be raised against the killing and the violence in Northern Ireland, just as we seek an end to brutality and repression everywhere. . . . Ulster is becoming Britain's Vietnam.

—*Senate address, October 20, 1971*

Perhaps never before in the history of the world has there been an emblem so full of the great aspirations of all men everywhere as the flag of the United States. . . . The flag our forebears received at their citizenship ceremony initiated them into the life of love and freedom, and they went forth to build a new nation. Our common aspirations today are as boundless as the mind of man. . . . They exceed even the deepest divisions of our time, because they reflect the timeless quest of men to be free, to live in a society that is open, where the principles of freedom and justice and equality prevail.

—*Fourth of July Address, Wakefield, MA, 1970*

Rarely if ever in our history have private-interest groups been better organized, better financed, or more resistant to the force of change. It was Lord Bryce who commented in the Nineteenth Century that American government was all engine and no brakes. Today it could be said . . . that our government is all brakes and no engine.

—*Speech, September 22, 1978*

What we do in the outside world must be based on a deep moral sense of our purpose as a nation. Without that sense of our enduring heritage— the values on which this nation was founded, the basic compassion and human concerns of our people—there is little we can do both for ourselves and for others. American involvement in the outside world must reflect what is best in our heritage and what is best in ourselves.

—*Speech, June 14, 1976*

ON THE CONSTITUTION AND
EQUAL JUSTICE UNDER LAW

IF TED KENNEDY HAD NOT BEEN A SENATOR, WHAT A great Supreme Court justice he might have made!

Looking over his lifetime of work, we find a dazzling array of writings on law and justice, many worthy of a legal scholar, but never as dusty and dry as the work so often found in academic journals.

He combined the scholar's breadth of knowledge with the advocate's passion, standing up for causes and principles in the style of a committed courtroom defender speaking for an embattled innocent. We saw this quality in him in the way he questioned nominees for attorney general who struck him as insufficiently committed to the preservation of our essential liberties. He took with utmost seriousness his charge as a senator to deliver to the president his best advice when it came to selection of justices for the highest court in the land; he would not consent to the appointment of anyone whose interpretation of the Constitution he found rigid and literalistic, unappreciative of the spirit of the founders' vision.

At the same time he courageously opposed movements, however popular they may have been, to tinker with the Constitution unnecessarily: He believed that the American flag stood for free speech and that an amendment to restrict that speech honors neither the flag nor the Constitution. Nor would he sit silent as opponents of gay rights proposed to write their hostility to gay relationships into the Constitution in the form of a "traditional marriage" amendment.

Each time the rights of a segment of our society have come under fire, Senator Kennedy was right there, returning fire—defending civil rights for racial minorities, civil liberties for victims of profiling, equality for women, fair treatment of immigrants— and kept at it, right till the end. John F. Kennedy once observed that "life is unfair," and that is certainly indisputable. But it is also true that life in America today is now to some degree a little less unfair due to his brother Teddy's lifetime of work for "justice for all."

Words [in the Constitution] are fine, but it has to be what a generation reads into those words.
—Speech to students
at Boston Latin Public High School,
April 29, 2002

Equal justice under law is not just a phrase carved in marble. It is the essence of the law, and the continuing challenge for our times is to see that it is a reality in our lives.
—Speech at the Judicial Conference
of the U.S. Court of Appeals for the First Circuit,
Washington, DC, September 13, 1993

The Constitution does not just protect those whose views we share; it also protects those with whose views we disagree.
—Letter to a constituent, 1997

Today, many of us are concerned about the preservation of basic liberties protected by the Constitution. Clearly, as we work together to bring terrorists to justice and enhance our security, we must also act to preserve and protect our Constitution. The ideals we stand for here at home and around the world are indispensable to our strength. We betray those ideals and we betray the Constitution when we support detention of U.S. citizens without legal counsel or fair judicial review, and mass registration and fingerprinting of Muslim and Arab visa holders.

—*Comments at the Senate Judiciary Hearing on "The War Against Terrorism," March 4, 2003*

The First Amendment is one of the great pillars of our freedom. As we wage the war on terrorism to protect the nation for the future, it is also our responsibility to protect the ideals that America stands for here at home and around the world. This is not the time to restrict fundamental constitutional rights. . . .

Freedom of the press is essential to the public's access to information. A free press is an important part of checks and balances on government and an important remedy for excess secrecy in government, and journalists have an indispensable role in fulfilling the public's right to know.

I remember a speech by Justice Bill Douglas when I was in law school. A student asked him what the most important export of the United States is. He said, without hesitation, "The First Amendment." The reason why is obvious. It gives life to the very concept of our democracy. It protects the freedoms of all Americans, including the right to criticize their government.

—Statement of support
for the Reporter Shield Bill,
July 20, 2005

If we set the precedent of limiting the First Amendment, in order to protect the sensibilities of those who are offended by flag burning, what will we say the next time someone is offended by some other minority view, or by some other person's exercise of the freedom the Constitution is supposed to protect?

—Letter to a constituent, 1997

As a nation we have no hereditary institutions, and a minimum of ceremonial schools. The Constitution itself is our national symbol—the symbol of our identity, our continuity, and also our diversity. It requires a mature people, mature in intelligence and political understanding, to respect that kind of abstract symbol, rather than the more tangible or human symbols of other nations.

—Speech, September 22, 1978

The checks and balances so vital to our democracy are what make our constitutional scheme the envy of the world and such a potent and enduring foundation for our democracy.

—Statement on Judicial Activism,
April 13, 2005

Civil rights is still the unfinished business of America, and we will not rest until we make Dr. King's dream a reality. We will not be satisfied until "justice rolls down like the waters and righteousness like a mighty stream."

—Martin Luther King Day Speech,
Boston, January 17, 2000

The separation of church and state can sometimes be frustrating for women and men of religious faith. They may be tempted to misuse government in order to impose a value which they cannot persuade others to accept. But once we succumb to that temptation, we step onto a slippery slope where everyone's freedom is at risk.

—Speech at Liberty University,
October 3, 1983

We need more effective safeguards to ensure that every American can fully exercise his constitutional right to privacy. We must protect Americans against the compiling of inaccurate or unverified data and the unrestricted use and dissemination of such data.

—Speech, June 12, 1974

A federal program is not the solution to every problem. But there continues to be an important federal role in solving the problems of our society by investing in people and the infrastructure needed for our country to succeed and our citizens to thrive. To believe otherwise is hostile to the basic values of our country and to the historic concept of "We the People" in our Constitution. We must not rob the people of the resource of government. It is *their* government and we must make it work for them.

—Speech, National Press Club,
Washington, DC, January 11, 1995

What we were, what we are, and what we shall be as a nation and as individuals are closely bound up with that single, simple phrase "Congress shall make no law abridging the freedom of speech."

—Speech, June 13, 1978

Diversity—*e pluribus unum*—"out of many, one," is not just a slogan on our coins but the founding political principle of our nation. Too often in those years [of the Reagan and Bush presidencies] it was replaced by the politics of division, and progress was far more difficult than it should have been.

—Remarks on civil rights, October 22, 1993

We know that the struggle for equality is not over. Even with affirmative action, there are significant racial disparities in higher education between minority students and white students. Currently, African-Americans enroll in higher education at 85% the rate of white students. Latinos enroll in higher education at only 80% the rate of white students. As a country, we need to work to close that gap not—as the Administration now proposes—to widen it.

—*Statement on Affirmative Action,*
January 15, 2003

I hope for an America where no president, no public official, no individual will ever be deemed a greater or lesser American because of religious doubt—or religious belief.

—*Speech at Liberty University,*
October 3, 1983

In light of the ideological-driven selection of judicial nominees, it would be wrong to ask Senators to ignore the nominee's ideology. Neither the constitution itself nor historical practice demands blindness to this ideological pattern of nominations. Judicial nominees who come before the Senate should have not only the qualifications and temperament to be a judge. They should also be committed to democratic principles and ideals. Nominees should respect our judicial system and the co-equal relationship between the executive, legislative, and judicial branches.

—*Remarks at the American Constitution Society's conference on "The State of the Judiciary," September 25, 2002*

The real transgression occurs when religion wants government to tell citizens how to live uniquely personal parts of their lives. The failure of Prohibition proves the futility of such an attempt when a majority or even a substantial minority happens to disagree. Some questions may be inherently individual ones, or people may be sharply divided about whether they are. In such cases, like Prohibition and abortion, the proper role of religion is to appeal to the conscience of the individual, not the coercive power of the state.

—*Speech at Liberty University, October 3, 1983*

We must end the continuing blatant discrimination in our voting laws. If I could, I would lock every door in the Supreme Court but one, and require all nine justices to enter every morning through the majestic main door above which are inscribed in marble the four simple, basic words that are the foundation of America and always will be: "Equal Justice Under Law." Because when we say "all," we must mean "all."

—Remarks on Martin Luther King, Jr. Holiday,
Peoples Congregational United Church of Christ,
January 14, 2001

Too often, "Equal Justice Under Law" has been reduced to an empty slogan for too many. It is wrong to leave people powerless against injustice because they can't afford the kind of justice that is there for the asking by the wealthy. A right without a remedy is no right at all.

—Remarks on Martin Luther King, Jr. Holiday,
Peoples Congregational United Church of Christ,
January 14, 2001

While economic growth is important to all Americans, it is absolutely essential for black Americans. It is the indispensible condition of black progress. Other groups may have achieved a level of comfort for themselves, but they have no right to stop the engines of growth before others have begun to board the train.

—Speech, May 7, 1978

Much remains to be done to secure equal opportunity for women. Enactment of the Equal Rights Amendment alone will not undo generations of economic injustice, but it will encourage women in all parts of the country in their efforts to obtain fairness under the nation's laws.

—Statement on the Equal Rights Amendment,
March 22, 2001

After two hundred years I think it is safe to say that women in America are now demanding full equality in every aspect of American life. And after two hundred years I think they have every right to expect it. Nor can this nation afford to deny it.

—Speech, May 18, 1976

In the rapid pace of society and its emphasis on youth and mobility, the handicapped have been left behind, relegated to the backwaters of society, ostracized by their contemporaries, victimized by unfair attitudes of discrimination.

—Speech, June 28, 1978

In June, in its landmark decision in *Lawrence v. Texas*, the Supreme Court struck down a Texas law that made homosexual conduct a crime. . . . Predictably, the Court's decision has been denounced by some of our colleagues in Congress. The Republican Policy Committee in the Senate recently published a paper declaring that the decision "gave aid and comfort" to "activist lawyers" who seek to "force same-sex marriage on society through pliant, activist courts." Only an amendment to the Constitution, the report states, can prevent this result. The Constitution is the foundation of our democracy. It reflects the enduring principles of our country. Notwithstanding the views of some of my Republican colleagues, the Constitution does not need a makeover.

—Remarks in opposition to a proposed
Constitutional amendment on the definition of
marriage, September 4, 2003

It's fundamentally wrong to discriminate against gays and lesbians by denying them the many benefits and protections that the laws of the state provide for married couples. Being part of a family is a basic right. It means having loved ones with whom to build a future, to share life's joys and tears. It means having the right to be treated fairly by the tax code, to visit loved ones in the hospital, and to receive health benefits, family leave benefits, and survivor benefits. I urge my colleagues to reject efforts to write that kind of bigotry into federal law.

—*Statement on equal rights for*
gays and lesbians, April 13, 2005

As far back as Justinian's Rome, criminal codes have been symbols of justice, examples of society's commitment to the principles of fairness. In this respect, the current federal criminal code is a disgrace. Congresses over the years have enacted some three thousand criminal laws, piling one on top of another until we have a structure that looks more like a Rube Goldberg contraption than a comprehensive criminal code.

—*Speech, January, 19, 1978*

We [in Congress] enacted the landmark Americans With Disabilities Act, bringing comprehensive protection for the rights of forty-three million Americans. Because of that law, fellow citizens across the country are finally learning that "disabled" does not mean "unable."

—Remarks on civil rights legislation,
October 22, 1993

Today we seek to take the next step on this journey of justice by banning discrimination based on sexual orientation. . . . We know we cannot change attitudes overnight. But the great lesson of American history is that changes in the law are an essential step in breaking down barriers of bigotry, exposing prejudice for what it is, and building a strong and fair nation.

—Statement on the Employment
Non-Discrimination Act of 1995

ON LEADERSHIP
AND COURAGE

ONE OF TED KENNEDY'S FORMATIVE EXPERIENCES WAS his meeting with the king and queen of England, who came to pay a call on his father, Joseph P. Kennedy, the newly appointed Ambassador to the Court of St. James, in the year before England's entry into World War II. Kennedy recalled having to be "gussied up" for the occasion. He was six years old. He had already met the young princess Elizabeth at Windsor Castle on a previous occasion. This marked the beginning of a lifetime of getting to know world leaders. There is hardly an important figure on the world scene in the past 60 years that Ted Kennedy has not met at one time or another. He spoke with Nelson Mandela just four days after his release from his 27-year imprisonment in South Africa; he has met with the heads of the world's great religions from the Pope to the Dalai Lama. Safe to say, then, that this was a man who knew leadership when he saw it. And often in his speeches he would cite examples of leadership, both from those he knew well and from those renowned in history.

But he was just as quick to recognize and pay tribute to the extraordinary leadership and courage of those whose names remain obscure. His 1999 eulogy for six firefighters from Worcester, Massachusetts, who gave their lives to save others, is as moving as any praise of Nobel Peace Prize winners.

He has also recognized the courage of lone dissenters, steadfast individuals who refuse to bow to the pressure of dictators or bureaucracies abroad, just as he has stood up for whistleblowers at home, people who refuse to bow to political pressure or self-interest to keep on doing what conscience tells them is right. At times Senator Kennedy has occupied this role himself. When the pundits of the media were all saying that liberalism was a dying creed and when so many other politicians were hastening to disassociate themselves from "the L-word," Senator Kennedy was one of the few not to edge away from his core beliefs. After the Republicans took control of both the House and the Senate in the mid-1990s, and tax-cutting and "small government" became all the rage, Senator Kennedy protested the end of effective programs that gave hope to the poor, so that the rich could pay less than their fair share. He stayed firm in his opposition to the death penalty when it was political risky to do so. In 1994, Republican Mitt Romney challenged him for his supposedly "safe" Senate seat, and for some months of the campaign, it was neck-and-neck between them in the polls. He was fighting for his political life.

Even so, he persisted in defending the civil liberties of despised groups, including undocumented immigrants and terrorism suspects in Guantanamo. He would not budge in his opposition to any justification for torture—it was immoral, and a disgrace to our American ideals, he said.

It was with this same courage and square-jawed determination that enabled him to live his life to the full in the face of his diagnosis of brain cancer. And, as he reports in his memoir, *True Compass*, he has been rewarded with a final year of life filled with faith, joy, and love.

The events of September 11th made clear that our nation's public safety officers are true heroes. While the pictures of tired, dust-covered fire fighters confronting unimaginable horror at the World Trade Center and the Pentagon are permanently emblazoned on our minds, so also is the memory of their strength and courage. We will never forget the example those brave men and women set that day. The dedication and resolve of fire fighters in the face of life-threatening danger truly represent the best in America.

—Speech at the Legislative Conference
of the International Association
of Fire Fighters, March 19, 2002

There is still much to learn by walking in [Dr. Martin Luther King's] path. His views are still timely. Nearly 33 years have passed, but readers today would think they are seeing the work of **the best** of today's social commentators. His great **speech** touches on many specific issues that are especially important now, such as education, economic opportunity, community reinvestment, affordable housing and home ownership.

He describes successful grassroots efforts that are still relevant models for today.

Most important, Dr. King reminds us that the effects of hundreds of years of slavery and segregation cannot be wiped away in a few years. The work goes on. Clearly, we've made remarkable progress since 1967, and all Americans owe Dr. King a tremendous debt of gratitude. But we are still fighting his fight for economic justice and full equality.

—*Speech at Boston's 7th Annual Tribute to Dr. Martin Luther King, Jr., January 17, 2000*

Today, our souls ache for the loss of James and Jeremiah, and Joseph and Paul, and Timothy and Thomas—six good and decent men, strong men and magnificent public servants, who gave their lives unselfishly and courageously in the line of duty.

Every day, they accepted the peril of their jobs with unflinching hearts and unwavering spirits. They faced dangers on a daily basis that few of us can even imagine. Time and time again, they battled fires, rescued children, saved lives and returned to the firehouse with the quiet pride of knowing that they truly did make the difference. Now they have gone to God, and we gather here to celebrate their lives and mourn their loss.

In these agonizing days, we draw strength from the message of hope they left behind. On the honor roll of heroes, these six deserve the highest laurels. In our quest to teach our children about character, we can point to each of them—their sacrifice, their commitment, their faith, their willingness to brave the odds.

—Eulogy for the six Worcester,
MA firemen killed in the line of duty,
December 9, 1999

I entered public life with a young President [his brother, John F. Kennedy] who inspired a generation and the world. It gives me great hope that as I leave, another young President inspires another generation and once more on America's behalf inspires the entire world.

—Letter to President Obama, May 12, 2009

Last night the nation paused to pay tribute to Rosa Parks, whose life and dedication to equal opportunity for each and every American will be forever written in the heart and souls of the nation and in the pages of our history. The light that shone in the Capitol last night cast its beams across the country. The tears of the Parks family were the tears of a nation that will remain eternally in the debt to this great woman who became a profile in courage for our time and all time. When Rosa Parks sat down half a century ago, America stood up. Her quiet fight for equality sounded the bells of freedom for millions and awakened the moral conscience of the nation. We will always remember that great December, when Rosa Parks sat alone, so that others could sit together.

—*Tribute to Rosa Parks, October 31, 2005*

He [Ronald Reagan] was always a good friend and a gracious foe. He wanted to defeat his opponents, but not destroy them.

—*Remarks about former President Reagan,*
April 2007 (quoted on Politico.com)

Individual faults and frailties are no excuse to give in—and no exemption from the common obligation to give of ourselves.

—Ted Kennedy quotation
read by President Barack Obama
as part of his eulogy
delivered at the funeral mass,
August 29, 2009.

The strength of the family is our greatest national treasure.

—Speech, May 26, 1976

We do not need more study. We do not need more analysis. We do not need more rhetoric. What we need is more leadership and commitment.

—Speech, July 27, 1972

It does not take a constitutional amendment to reduce the federal deficit or balance the federal budget. All it takes is enough courage by Congress and the administration to make the tough decisions we're elected to make. If we're not willing to balance the budget, the Constitution can't do it for us.

—Statement opposing the Balanced Budget Amendment, March 1, 1994

The challenges we face will require important changes in the structure of our institutions. It will not be easy to fit these changes into old categories, liberal or conservative, radical or reactionary. Instead, they will bring to our public life new meanings for old words in our political dialogue—words such as "power," "community," and "purpose."

—Speech, May 14, 1978

If Democrats run for cover, if we become pale carbon copies of the opposition and try to act like Republicans, we will lose—and deserve to lose. . . . Democrats must be more than warmed-over Republicans. The last thing this country needs is two Republican parties.

—Speech at the National Press Club, January 11, 1995, shortly before the swearing-in of the new Congress under Republican control

The most troublesome questions confronting Americans do not have Republican answers or Democratic answers. . . . They have human answers, and American answers, for they are the questions that ask what kind of life we want to lead and what kind of nation we want to have.

—Commencement address,
Manhattanville College, June 12, 1970

This Administration has had its chance—and it failed the basic test of competence. It failed to deploy adequate focus in Iraq to win the peace. It failed at Abu Ghraib. It failed in granting sweetheart deals to Halliburton. It has failed the loss-of-confidence test, the basic test of Presidential leadership.

—Remarks on the Senate floor
on the Bush Administration's
multiple failures of leadership in Iraq,
September 10, 2004

Part of the larger challenge we face is that Congress is a crisis-oriented institution, with few mechanisms and little inclination to deal with problems before they become acute. . . . We need better distant early warning signals, better mechanisms and institutional arrangements for handling problems which are not yet brush fires, but which are already smoldering and may well cause the conflagrations of the future.

—Speech, April 30, 1979

Dissent, like so many other things in the America of 1970, has become too comfortable. It takes five minutes to draw the letters on a protest sign, but it takes a lifetime of dedicated service to make a contribution to society.

—Distinguished Lecture Series,
Boston University, September 15, 1970

The person who serves as Attorney General must inspire the trust and respect of all Americans. Inscribed in stone over the center entrance to the Department of Justice is this phrase—"The Place of Justice Is a Hallowed Place." All Americans deserve to have confidence that when the next Attorney General walks through the doors of Justice and into that hallowed place, he will be serving them too. On the basis of his record, tens of millions of Americans can have no such confidence. I therefore oppose this nomination.

—Judiciary Committee Executive Business Meeting on the Confirmation of Senator John Ashcroft for Attorney General, January 30, 2001

America still has considerable work to do to improve the lives of our African American citizens. Civil rights is still the great unfinished business of our nation. But African Americans and all Americans are better off today because Martin Luther King challenged this country in the 1960s. As Dr. King said: Cowardice asks the question "Is it safe?" Expediency asks the question "Is it politic?" Vanity asks the question "Is it popular?" But conscience asks the question "Is it right?" And there comes a time when one must take a position that is neither safe nor politic nor popular, but he must take it because conscience tells him it is right.

—Presentation of the 2000 Robert F. Kennedy Human Rights Award, November 21, 2000

Jackie Robinson's career and courage symbolize the inspiring words of our national anthem that he and the nation heard each time a baseball game was about to begin—"the land of the free, and the home of the brave." But in those days, millions of Americans were not free, no matter how brave they were.

Jackie Robinson was a miracle worker who helped change all that. Athletically, he was in a class by himself. At UCLA in 1941, he became the first athlete in the history of the university—and to this day still the only one—to earn a letter in four sports in the same year. In 1949, his second year with the Dodgers, he was named the National League's Most Valuable Player. And when his all-too-brief Major League career ended after 10 seasons, he was elected to the Baseball Hall of Fame on the first ballot.

—Press Conference following the award
of the Congressional Gold Medal
to Jackie Robinson,
April 30, 2003

In an area where our founding fathers failed—the founding fathers wrote slavery into the Constitution—we fought a civil war, but it wasn't really until we had Dr. King and Coretta Scott King in the '50s that awakened the conscience of the nation, so the political leadership of the early '60s could begin what I call the march to progress, that of knocking down walls of discrimination on race, religion, ethnicity and gender, and disability. And we have benefited so much from their leadership and from their inspiration.

—Response to an interview question on "The Early Show," CBS, January 31, 2006

September 11th—that horrible and hateful day—has scorched our minds, our memories, and our hearts.

Our lives were forever changed. And in the days and the weeks since that hideous crime, our entire nation has continued to mourn the thousands of innocent victims of those cruel and heartless attacks.

We come together today in Boston to remember the friends and family members from our own state whose lives were cut short without reason or sense on that fateful day, and to offer comfort and our prayers to try to ease the pain of those left behind.

It is especially fitting that we gather here in Faneuil Hall, this magnificent landmark of liberty, which for two centuries has been the symbol of our nation's freedom. This hallowed hall is a monument to those who dedicated their lives, their fortunes and their sacred honor to the early struggles for liberty and justice in this great land of America. The friends and loved ones we mourn today were able to pursue their own dreams and their own happiness because of that early hard-won freedom. And they themselves have become martyrs for liberty and justice in our own time.

—*Massachusetts Memorial: A Celebration of Life,*
Faneuil Hall, Boston,
November 16, 2001

In the aftermath of these shameful attacks, there is understandable anger across the nation. But it is wrong and irresponsible to jump to conclusions and make false accusations against Arabs and Muslims in our communities. Above all, we must guard against any acts of violence based on such bigotry. America's ideals are under attack too, and we must do all we can to uphold them at this difficult time.

—*Remarks on September 13, 2001,*
in support of U.S. Muslim and Arab
communities in the aftermath
of the September 11 terrorist attacks

I don't think you're going to be a success in anything if you think about losing, whether it's in sports or in politics.

—*Quoted in* Sportswit *by Lee Green, 1984*

ON THE KENNEDY FAMILY
AND ITS LEGACY

EDWARD MOORE KENNEDY WAS THE YOUNGEST OF NINE children, born into a family already famous enough for the birth of their fourth son to merit not a small birth announcement in the local newspaper, but a full column-length news article in *each* of the two competing Boston dailies.

Throughout his 77 years he was constantly surrounded by family: He was father to three, stepfather to two, grandfather to four, and uncle to more than two dozen, including Bobby's eleven children and Jack's two children, all left fatherless by assassins and for whom he was an active father substitute. As he told *New York Times* reporter Fox Butterfield in an interview in October, 1992, "Thankfully, I've been inundated with children all my life."

With a lifetime of being part of a large and celebrated family, one can either try to escape it and strike out alone, or embrace it wholeheartedly, seeking refuge and support from its numerous members. With Ted Kennedy the path was clear: His love and reliance on his family is something noted by all.

Yet one of the most significant moments of his life, that he identifies as such in his memoir, *True Compass*, ended with a recognition of distinctiveness from his family, of his longing for a chance to be just himself, not "a Kennedy." He had just won reelection to the Senate in what turned out to be hard-fought campaign against Republican challenger Mitt Romney in 1994. In his victory speech that night he gave full credit to his family, who, as always, had rallied around him and campaigned hard on his behalf: "Well, this victory isn't really about me. It's about my family and about the people of Massachusetts and their residual goodwill that goes all the way back to Grandpa's day—" Suddenly, his wife Vicki interrupted with a truth that he needed to hear: "You know, Teddy, if you had lost, it would've been *you* that lost. It wouldn't have been your family . . ." So, she concluded, "*You* won! Not your family. *You.*"

This, says Ted Kennedy, was something he had yearned all his life to hear. And it took a new family member, his second wife, Victoria Reggie Kennedy, to see it.

Like my brothers before me, I pick up the fallen standard. Sustained by the memory of our priceless years together, I shall try to carry forward that special commitment to justice, to excellence, and to courage that distinguished their lives.

—Speech given before the start of the
1968 Democratic Convention

I think about my brothers every day.
—Interview with Reuters, 2006

We loved him [Robert Kennedy] as a brother, and as a father, and as a son. From his parents, and from his older brothers and sisters—Joe and Kathleen and Jack—he received an inspiration which he passed on to all of us. He gave us strength in time of trouble, wisdom in time of uncertainty, and sharing in time of happiness. He will always be by our side.

Love is not an easy feeling to put into words. Nor is loyalty, or trust, or joy. But he was all of these. He loved life completely and he lived it intensely.

—Eulogy for Robert Kennedy,
St. Patrick's Cathedral, New York,
June 8, 1968

My brother need not be idealized, or enlarged in death beyond what he was in life; to be remembered simply as a good and decent man, who saw wrong and tried to right it, saw suffering and tried to heal it, saw war and tried to stop it. Those of us who loved him and who take him to his rest today, pray that what he was to us, and what he wished for others, will some day come to pass for all the world. As he said many times, in many parts of this nation, to those he touched and who sought to touch him: "Some men see things as they are and say why. I dream things that never were and say why not."

—Eulogy for Robert Kennedy,
St. Patrick's Cathedral, New York,,
June 8, 1968

I often think of what she [Jackie] said about Jack in December after he died: "They made him a legend, when he would have preferred to be a man." Jackie would have preferred to be just herself, but the world insisted that she be a legend too.

—Eulogy for his sister-in-law,
Jacqueline Kennedy Onassis, May 23, 1994

John [Kennedy, Jr.] was a serious man who brightened our lives with his smile and his grace. He was a son of privilege who founded a program called Reaching Up to train better caregivers for the mentally disabled. He joined Wall Street executives on the Robin Hood Foundation to help the city's impoverished children. And he did it all so quietly, without ever calling attention to himself. John was one of Jackie's two miracles. He was still becoming the person he would be, and doing it by the beat of his own drummer. He had only just begun. There was in him a great promise of things to come.

The Irish Ambassador recited a poem to John's father and mother soon after John was born. I can hear it again now, at this different and difficult moment:

"We wish to the new child
A heart that can be beguiled
By a flower that the wind lifts as it passes.
If the storms break for him
May the trees shake for him
Their blossoms down.
In the night that he is troubled
May a friend wake for him

So that his time be doubled,
And at the end of all loving and love
May the Man above
Give him a crown."

—*Eulogy for his nephew,*
John F. Kennedy, Jr.,
July 1999

Rose [his mother] is the finest teacher we ever had. She made our home a university that surpassed any formal classroom in the exciting quest for knowledge. With her gentle games and questions, she could bring the farthest reaches of the university to our dinner table, or transform the daily headlines into new and exciting adventures in understanding.

—*Speech at Georgetown University,*
October 1, 1977

The thing about being a Kennedy is that you come to know that there's a time for the Kennedys. And it's hard to know when that time is, or if it will ever come again.

—*Quoted in* Time *magazine, January 10, 1969*

John Kennedy referred to the age in which we live—an age when history moves with the tramp of earthquake feet, an age when a handful of men and nations have the power literally to devastate mankind. But he did not speak in despair or with a sense of hopelessness.

—*Speech, Trinity College Historical Society Bicentennial, Dublin, Ireland, March 3, 1970*

From my vantage point as the youngest of the nine Kennedy children, my family did not so much live in the world as comprise the world. Though I have long since outgrown that simplistic view, I have never questioned its emotional truth. We depended on one another. We savored food and music and laughter with one another. We learned from and taught one another. We worshipped one another. We loved one another. We were mutually loyal, even as we were mutually competitive, with an intensity that owed more to joy than to an urge for domination. These values flowed into us on the energies of Joseph and Rose Kennedy.

—True Compass: A Memoir, *2009*

From the windows of my office in Boston . . . I can see the Golden Stairs from Boston Harbor where all eight of my great-grandparents set foot on this great land for the first time. That immigrant spirit of limitless possibility animates America even today.

—From a Senate speech in 2007, quoted by reporter Kathy Kiely in USA Today, *August 26, 2009*

A VOICE FOR CHILDREN

IT'S EASY ENOUGH TO POINT OUT HOW MUCH SENATOR Kennedy has done for children. Just take it from Reg Weaver, former president of the National Education Association: "Every major education law passed since the 1960s has borne Kennedy's imprint, from Head Start to the Elementary and Secondary Education Act. He has proven himself, time and again, to be a fighter for children." (Weaver was quoted on Air America's website.)

Just count up the seven million formerly uninsured children now covered by health insurance through the S-CHIP program that came into being in 1997 due to Kennedy's authorship of the State Children's Health Insurance Program legislation and was expanded in 2009.

Look at the accolades bestowed on him by one of the oldest and most respected children's health organizations: In 2001 the March of Dimes Foundation gave him its top honor, the Franklin Delano Roosevelt Award, for his advocacy of children's health issues, and then in 2003 and again in 2007 gave him its Public Affairs Leadership Award as the outstanding member of Congress in the field of maternal and child health.

There's much more of the same, of course. It would have been easy for him at any point to say to himself that he'd done as much as he could for children, and slow down, and pass the baton. But that wasn't his way. Up until his final weeks he was hard at work on new legislation, pushing for greater expansion of several of the children's programs that he had helped to bring into being, to make sure that even more kids would be served.

President Obama has promised to push for passage of those bills now that his friend Ted Kennedy is no longer here to do so.

Our nation's greatest resource is its children. We must do all we can to ensure that they reach their full potential. Improving school readiness is an essential first step.

—Introduction to the Early Learning Trust Fund,
March 25, 1999

Education shouldn't have to be an obstacle course. Imagine how much more you could accomplish without the albatross of overcrowded and outdated facilities.

—Speech at Edward Everett Elementary School,
Dorchester, MA, March 29, 1999

The greatest tribute of all to Dr. Seuss is a child who learns to read. He'd be very impressed by the 3rd graders here at Squantum. What a wonderful slogan you have—"Drop Everything and Read" for at least 15 minutes a day. Every child in America should do that. Dr. Seuss would love it—and so would the whole country.

—Statement on "Read Across America,"
March 1, 1999

It is the young who have often been the first to speak and act against injustice or corruption and tyranny, wherever it is found. More than any other group in the population, it is the young who refuse to allow a difficulty or a challenge to become an excuse to fail to meet it. We need their ideas and ideals, the spirit and dedication of young Americans who are willing to hold a mirror to society and probe the sores that others would ignore.

—Speech, February 9, 1976

There are many who criticize youth for not being more obedient to our traditions. What they fail to understand is that the questions of our youth are disturbing because they are questions we ourselves find hard to answer. They are questions we ourselves refuse to face.

—Speech to the National Council for Social Studies, April 11, 1970

If there are some children in this land—whether because they are black or because they were born on a reservation or because they are poor—if there are some children who do not have an equal opportunity for a quality education, then there are some children who are not free.

—*Speech, April 25, 1977*

In the generation of our fathers and grandfathers, schools were expected to produce only a few leaders. Their principal output was unskilled workers. During that era, managers and professionals were all too often members of an elite class. The fantastically rapid development of modern technology has changed all that. The call of new opportunity has gone out to millions of American youth, and our education system must respond.

—*Speech at the Conference of the National Council for Social Studies, April 11, 1970*

Every generation has its own mission in the life of the nation. Your generation may well be the peace generation, because the issue of nuclear war or peace will in all likelihood be settled by you.

—Address at the Brown University Commencement Forum, June 4, 1983

Good schools and good teachers are every bit as important to the future strength of our country as a strong defense.

—Comments at a committee hearing, September 10, 2002

There has been a steady drumbeat of loud calls for cutting welfare benefits by some in this Congress. But there has been a deafening silence on the need for child care. It is time to break the silence and put together a realistic reform— reform based not on rhetoric but on results.

—Statement on welfare reform, March 1, 1995

We must invest more in early education and healthy development for the youngest children, so that entering school ready to learn is no longer just a hollow mantra but a genuine reality. . . . If we fail to meet a child's development needs starting at birth, we fail not only the child, but our country and our future as well.

—Address at the National Press Club,
Washington, DC, January 12, 2005

We all agree that no child should be left behind— regardless of background, race, or gender, or whether a child is homeless, a child of a migrant worker, or an immigrant. Every child has the right to a high-quality education and every qualified student should be able to afford to go to college. But we cannot call for reform, then refuse to pay the bill. Parents and children deserve a guarantee, not a federal IOU.

—Statement on the Bush education budget,
March 29, 2001

For our many young people today who have grown up in a drug culture and are experimenting with drugs, the emphasis should be on prevention and rehabilitation, not simply throwing them in jail. We should not automatically burden these youngsters with the albatross of a criminal felony to wear for the rest of their lives.

—Statement, October 7, 1970

America does more today to regulate the safety of toy guns than real guns—and it is a national disgrace. When we listen to what unnecessary and preventable gun violence has done to the victims here today, we know that action is urgently needed. Practical steps can clearly be taken to protect children more effectively from guns, and to achieve greater responsibility by parents, gun manufacturers, and gun dealers. This legislation calls for such steps—and it deserves to be enacted this year by Congress.

—Introduction to legislation on
Children's Gun Violence
on the first anniversary of the
Jonesboro School Shooting,
March 24, 1999

It is wrong—dead wrong—to grant oversized tax breaks for the wealthiest Americans, but fail to invest more in our nation's public schools. What we need is not just a tax cut, but an economic plan that responds to today's shaky economy by helping all Americans get a good education and good jobs. If we expect our children to succeed in the 21st century economy, we must do better. If we expect our schools to meet the challenges of a modern education for all of our children, we must do more.

—Press conference on the Bush education budget,
March 20, 2001

Today, by the time they enter school, the average child will have watched 4,000 hours of television. That is roughly the equivalent of four years of school. For far too many youngsters, this is wasted time—time consuming "empty calories" for the brain. Instead, that time could be spent reading, writing, and learning. Through Ready to Learn television programming, children can obtain substantial educational benefits that turn TV time into learning time.

—Statement on the Ready to Learn,
Ready to Teach Act of 2001, March 22, 2001

The most important relationship in children's lives is the one with their parents. It is absolutely essential to a child's future that the parent-child relationship be as positive as possible. Without a close, dependable relationship, a child's potential can be severely and permanently impaired. It's essential to provide high quality education and support not only for children, but also for their parents.

There are few better ways to show children you care than to take the time each day to read with them. When children have books and adults who read to them an early age, they acquire better language skills and learn to love and appreciate books.

—White House Summit on
Early Childhood Cognitive Development,
July 26, 2001

We want every child to be welcomed into a loving home, and to be part of the American Dream. This fundamental vision is at the heart of who we are as Democrats, and we must do everything in our power to make it a reality.

—Address at the National Press Club,
Washington, DC, January 12, 2005

ISSUES OF GLOBAL IMPACT:
THE ENVIRONMENT, WAR, NATIONAL SECURITY, AND PUBLIC SAFETY

TAKE ANY ISSUE OF GLOBAL IMPACT AND RESEARCH TED Kennedy's position on it. It doesn't matter what it is-whether it's something that's long been on the public radar, like the environment, or some obscure trade issue, like changing tariffs on imported shoes—and somewhere in the vast body of the Senator's speeches and writings, you will find he took a stand on it. And not just a pro forma stand, a nod to the conventional wisdom on the subject, but much more: He put his topnotch staff to work and thoroughly researched the issue. His positions never seemed hastily thrown together or done as a "You support my issue and I'll support yours" favor to a fellow politician. When you read a policy statement, you find that the facts are right, the implications are thought through, and the position based on logic—although it may well be argued with passion.

What kinds of issues merit this attention? Here's a very abridged list: energy conservation, environmental protection, combating the spread of terrorism, nuclear arms control, gun control, equity in global trade, charting a path to peace in the Middle East, dealing with Iran, the war in Iraq, the war in Afghanistan, ethnic slaughter in Darfur, human rights in China, the push for democracy in the former Soviet republics, and the global fight against AIDS.

We know we have shortchanged the Senator by the brevity of this list but we know that to do him full justice would use up a lot more paper—and that brings up yet another cause dear to his heart: saving trees.

People are beginning to realize that we are a part of nature, not outside it. We are beginning to understand that instead of conquering nature, we must live in harmony with it.

—*Speech, January 3, 1970*

Our fragile planet is not a Republican or Democratic or American community. It is a world community, and we forget that truth at our very, very great peril.

—*Address at the National Press Club, Washington, DC, January 12, 2005*

It's better to send in the Peace Corps than the Marine Corps.

—*Quoted in "Famous Sayings" compiled by Wordpress.com*

National security begins at home. It begins on the streets and sidewalks of our cities. It begins in the small towns and villages of our country. It begins on the farms in our rural areas. These are the places where the first two hundred years of our nation were decided. And these are the places where the fate of America is going to be decided in the third century of our history.

—Speech, March 1, 1976

There is no priority for this nation higher than guaranteeing our national security and safety. Without an effective military force, and without a worldwide understanding that we have the unwavering will to use this force when our national interests are in danger, we unnecessarily place our way of life in peril.

—Speech, June 3, 1969

As we seek to improve the world in which we live and to secure its people against the scourge of war and want, we must understand that peace is not a final victory but a continual effort.

—Speech, December 2, 1975

For half a century, our policy has been to do everything we possibly can to prevent nuclear war. And so far, we've succeeded. The hard-liners say things are different today. A nuclear war won't be so bad if we just make the nukes a little smaller. We'll call them mini-nukes. They're not real nukes. A little nuclear war's O.K. That's nonsense. Nuclear war is nuclear war is nuclear war. We don't want it anywhere, anytime, anyplace. Make no mistake. A mini-nuke is still a nuke.

Is half a Hiroshima O.K.? Is a quarter of a Hiroshima O.K.? Is a little mushroom cloud O.K.? That's absurd.

—Pressing for the continuation of the ban on low-yield nuclear weapons, May 20, 2003

The American people do not accept a chessboard view of the world, based only on power politics. Our policy must have a surer foundation, grounded in our basic humanitarian values as a nation.

—Speech, May 27, 1976

We learned a generation ago that the two broad oceans offer no real military security. Now we are learning that our economy is also not isolated from the harsh winds of change that are sweeping the world. American jobs, American prices, and American incomes are vitally affected by what happens abroad.

—*Speech, February 17, 1975*

Like December 7, 1941, September 11, 2001 will be remembered as a day that will live in infamy. Just as the Pearl Harbor attack galvanized the American people in their resolve to prevail in the war against fascism and tyranny, I am confident that yesterday's attack on the American people will galvanize our citizens and strengthen our spirit to prevail in the ongoing war against global terrorism. It is tragic that these criminals were able to succeed in carrying out the most brutal terrorist attack in history on American soil. I pledge to work with the President, the Congress, and the families of the victims to seek answers to the many questions that exist, and to do all we can to strengthen the security of our people and to prevent such atrocities in the future. The

American flag flies high today, and so does our commitment to our ideals here at home and all around the world.

> —*Statement on the Terrorist Attacks in New York and Washington, DC, September 12, 2001*

The life-and-death issue of war and peace is too important to be left to politics. And I disagree with those who suggest that this fateful issue cannot or should not be contested vigorously, publicly, and all across America. When it is the people's sons and daughters who will risk and even lose their lives, then the people should hear and be heard, speak and be listened to.

> —*Remarks on September 27, 2002, during the build-up before the U.S. invasion of Iraq*

The armed services continue to be a critical and worthwhile career for America's young men and women. If anything, it is now even more important for people of high caliber, committed to the nation's future, to serve in the armed forces.

—Speech, February 17, 1975

The coldly premeditated nature of preventive attacks and preventive wars makes them anathema to well-established international principles against aggression. Pearl Harbor has been rightfully recorded in history as an act of dishonorable treachery.

—Response to the Bush Doctrine
of Pre-emptive Attack,
October 7, 2002

The Administration's doctrine is a call for 21st century American imperialism that no other nation can or should accept. It is the antithesis of all that America has worked so hard to achieve in international relations since the end of World War II. This is not just an academic debate. There are important real-world consequences. A shift in our policy toward preventive war would reinforce the perception of America as a "bully" in the Middle East, and would fuel anti-American sentiment throughout the Islamic world and beyond. It would also send a signal to governments the world over that the rules of aggression have changed for them too, which could increase the risk of conflict between countries such as Russia and Georgia, India and Pakistan, and China and Taiwan.

—*Response to the Bush Doctrine*
of Pre-emptive Attack,
October 7, 2002

Based on some estimates, guns are statistically like rats: They outnumber our population. Not surprisingly, our output of ammunition for civilian firearms almost staggers the imagination. American industry outdoes all other nations in the production of bullets. . . . All of those bullets could not only wipe out the world's entire human population but destroy much of the world's wildlife as well.

—*Address to the Businessmen's Executive Movement for Peace in Vietnam, February 17, 1971*

America has a massive gun problem. The crisis is especially serious for children. In one year, firearms killed no children in Japan, 19 in Great Britain, 109 in France, 153 in Canada, and 5,285 children in the United States. For every child in the United States killed with a gun, four more are wounded. The overall rate of firearm-related deaths for American children is nearly twelve times greater than in twenty-five other industrial countries. Yet, the nation's response to this death toll has been minimal, and little has changed in our approach to regulating guns since 1973.

—Remarks in opposition to legal immunity for the gun industry, February 25, 2004

How ironic that many of the same individuals who are fighting to repeal federal support for higher education are also fighting to repeal the assault weapons ban and make those deadly weapons available on the streets and neighborhoods of cities across America. Do they think we have too many college students in our communities but not enough guns? We have often heard that the pen is mightier than the sword. I guess they now feel that the pen is more dangerous than a semiautomatic machine gun.

—Statement to the College Democrats of America, 1995

Terrorists are exploiting weaknesses and loopholes in the nation's gun laws. A terrorist manual found in Kabul instructed members of al Qaeda on how to purchase firearms legally in the United States. A member of the terrorist group Hezbollah was recently convicted in Detroit of weapons charges and conspiracy to ship weapons and ammunition to Lebanon; he had purchased many of the weapons at gun shows in Michigan. In 1999, a member of the Irish Republican Army spent more than $18,000 in South Florida purchasing dozens of handguns, rifles, and ammunition, which he then attempted to ship to Ireland. That same year, only a lack of cash prevented two domestic terrorists from purchasing a grenade launcher at a gun show, for the purpose of blowing up two large propane tanks in suburban Sacramento.

Enough is enough.

It is also essential to do all we can to keep guns out of the hands of terrorists. To achieve this goal, we should require background checks for all firearm purchases. . . . The "gun show loophole," however, makes a mockery of other restrictions by allowing terrorists and other criminals to make illegal firearm purchases at gun shows—no questions asked. It is long past time that we close it.

> —*Statement on the release of a report on guns and terror by the Brady Campaign, December 19, 2001*

The city of Hiroshima stands as more than a monument to massive death and destruction. It stands as a living testament to the necessity for progress toward nuclear disarmament.

> —*Speech, January 11, 1978*

The sad reality is that the course, the pace, and the objectives of arms control policies have been more influenced by the arms producers than by the arms controllers.

> —*Speech, December 2, 1975*

Tragically, the world's oldest civilization and the world's most modern civilization, the world's most populous nation and the world's richest and most powerful nation, glare at each other across the abyss of nuclear war. We should proclaim our willingness to adopt a new policy toward China, a policy of peace, today's reality, that encourages tomorrow's possibility.

—Statement to National Committee on
United States-China Relations,
New York City, March 20, 1969

Time and time again, it has been the people of Israel who have shown the courage, the genius, and the determination to give substance to their dreams. Coming together from their roots in a dozen nations, they have vindicated the faith of their forebears. They are part of the biblical prophecy, the prophecy that "I will bring them out from the peoples, and will gather them out of the countries, and will bring them to their own land."

—Speech, January 13, 1975

The policy failure in Iran was massive, ranging from our intelligence to our commerce, diplomacy, and strategy. As a result, we lost major opportunities for modernization, moderation, and stability in the region. In vain, despite the lessons of Vietnam, we poured virtually unlimited supplies of arms into Iran, in the hope that bombs and tanks and planes could somehow ensure the flow of oil to American homes and factories.

—Speech, April 2, 1979

There will be discussion in Washington and around the world about whether the ethnic violence in Darfur is, in fact, genocide, but we cannot allow the debate over definitions to obstruct our ability to act as soon as possible. It is a matter of the highest moral responsibility for each of us individually, for Congress, for the United States, and for the global community to do all we can to stop the violence against innocents in Darfur. We must act, because thousands of people's lives will be lost if we don't.

—Call for U.S. action to help stop the ethnic violence in Darfur, Sudan, April 29, 2004

I don't think America can just drill itself out of its current energy situation. We don't need to destroy the environment to meet our energy needs. We need smart, comprehensive, common-sense approaches that balance the need to increase domestic energy supplies with the need to maximize energy efficiency.

—*Statement on New Long-Term Energy Solutions,*
March 22, 2001

We should stop the non-scientific, pseudo-scientific, and anti-scientific nonsense emanating from the right wing, and start demanding immediate action to reduce global warming and prevent catastrophic climate change that may be on our horizon now. We must not let the [Bush] Administration distort science and rewrite and manipulate scientific reports in other areas. We must not let it turn the Environmental Protection Agency into the Environmental Pollution Agency.

—*Address to the National Press Club,*
Washington, DC, January 12, 2005

In strengthening security at our borders, we must also safeguard the unobstructed entry of the more than 31 million persons who enter the U.S. legally each year as visitors, students, and temporary workers. Many of them cross our borders from Canada and Mexico to conduct daily business or visit close family members.

We also must live up to our history and heritage as a nation of immigrants. Continued immigration is part of our national well-being, our identity as a nation, and our strength in today's world. In defending America, we are also defending the fundamental constitutional principles that have made America strong in the past and will make us even stronger in the future.

Our action must strike a careful balance between protecting civil liberties and providing the means for law enforcement to identify, apprehend and detain potential terrorists. It makes no sense to enact reforms that severely limit immigration into the United States. "Fortress America," even if it could be achieved, is an inadequate and ineffective response to the terrorist threat.

—Statement on the Introduction of the Enhanced Border Security and Visa Entry Reform Act of 2001, November 30, 2001

DEMOCRACY AND
HUMAN RIGHTS

TED KENNEDY WAS BOTH A BIG "D" DEMOCRAT AND A small "d" democrat. That is to say, he was both a ferocious defender of his party and a deep believer in the virtues of a system in which the people choose their leaders. He was also an astute observer of the way democracies function and how they are sometimes ill-served by overly partisan politics or by majority rule at the expense of minority rights. He critiqued the workings of democracy, both at home and abroad, and was even more vocal when it came to his appraisal of countries like China, which lack democracy, or post-Soviet Russia, where democratic practices have too often been compromised or abridged.

The big risk to democracy at home, as the senator has pointed out, comes when politicians put themselves ahead of the public interest or are not honest with the voters. Democracy's lifeblood is an educated and informed electorate, able to keep track of politicians' deeds, able to call them to account when they say one thing but do another. In that way democracy is dependent upon both a free press and the freedom of its citizens to follow their own conscience when those in power would have them bend to the majority's will.

Democracy without human rights is the tyranny of the majority. That may be better than the tyranny of an individual dictator, but it's a difference of scale, not principle.

Ted Kennedy was never one to shrink from criticizing an undemocratic action wherever he saw it, whether in foreign governments, in his own government, or yes, even occasionally in his own party, the Democrats with a capital D.

Integrity is the lifeblood of democracy. Deceit is a poison in its veins.
—*Speech at the Brookings Institution,*
April 5, 2004

The American people care deeply about human rights around the world. But they also believe that human rights begin at home.

—*Speech, June 9, 1977*

The more our feelings diverge, the more deeply felt they are, the greater is our obligation to grant the sincerity and essential decency of our fellow citizens on the other side.

—*Speech at Liberty University,*
October 3, 1983

[America is] not a continent, not an arsenal, not wealth and factories—but a democratic republic. Call it democracy or freedom, call it human liberty or individual opportunity, equality or justice, but underneath they are all the same— the belief in the right and capacity of every individual to govern himself and to share in governing the necessary institutions of social order.

—*Speech, May 14, 1978*

Community service is not a new idea in America. It is the essence of democracy. Throughout our history, we have dealt most effectively with the issues facing our country when we have come together to help one another.

—Statement at the Senate Judiciary Committee hearing for the Martin Luther King Holiday and Service Act, April 13, 1994

Citizenship is far more than just voting every two years or four years. The strength and genius of our democracy depends on the caring and involvement of our people, and we cannot truly secure our freedom without appealing to the character of our citizens. If we fail, we open the way for abuses of power in the hands of the few, for neglect of poverty and bigotry, and for arrogant foreign policies that shatter our alliances and make enemies of our friends.

—Address to the National Press Club, Washington, DC, January 12, 2005

Public education is one of the finest achievements of American democracy.

*—Press conference on the Bush
education budget, March 20, 2001*

Hate crimes are a national disgrace—an attack on everything this country stands for. They send a poisonous message that some Americans are second class citizens who deserve to be victimized solely because of their race, their ethnic background, their religion, their sexual orientation, their gender or their disability. These senseless crimes have a destructive and devastating impact not only on individual victims, but entire communities. If America is to live up to its founding ideals of liberty and justice for all, combating hate crimes must be a national priority.

*—Statement on Hate Crimes Prevention
Legislation, March 27, 2001*

One of the basic assumptions of our political system is that large centers of unaccountable power are inconsistent with democratic government and the values of a free society. If there is a single theme that ties together the best in both liberal and conservative political traditions, it is this hostility to unchecked power. If the awesome power of giant corporations is no longer adequately checked by the discipline of the market, it is not just our pocketbook that is in jeopardy, it is our liberty.

—*Speech, May 3, 1977*

Public financing of elections is the wisest possible investment that American taxpayers can make in the future of their country.

—*Speech, May 5, 1977*

Too often in recent years we have allowed debates on major issues to be polarized beyond the point of no return. We cannot afford to let bad debate drive out the good.

—*Speech, November 2, 1975*

Our large cities are totally impersonal: They crank human beings through their daily activities. Our large universities are totally impersonal: They stamp out people with fixed credentials. Our large industries are totally impersonal: They employ people in repetitive tasks empty of a sense of value. Our large units of government are totally impersonal: They exist for their own sake rather than for the people they serve. And all these institutions seem unresponsive to the individual complaint or desire. There is a general sense of helplessness, a feeling of uselessness.

> —*Acceptance speech for nomination as a*
> *candidate for re-election to the U.S. Senate*
> *at the Massachusetts Democratic Convention,*
> *Amherst, June 12, 1970*

Earlier this week, scientists announced the completion of a task that once seemed unimaginable—deciphering the entire DNA sequence of the human genetic code. This amazing accomplishment is likely to affect the 21st century as profoundly as the invention of the computer or the splitting of the atom affected the 20th century. The 21st century may well be the century of the life sciences, and nothing makes that point more clearly than this momentous discovery.

These new discoveries bring with them remarkable new opportunities for improving health care. But they also carry the danger that genetic information will be used, not to improve the lives of Americans, but as a basis for discrimination. Genetic discrimination may sound like something new and hard to understand, but it's not. Discrimination on the basis of a person's genetic traits is as unacceptable as discrimination on the basis of gender, skin color, or any other unalterable condition of a person's birth. Genetic discrimination is wrong, whether it takes place on a job application or in the office of an insurance underwriter.

—*Statement on Genetic Discrimination,*
June 29, 2000

Policy formation without public participation is like faith and hope without charity.

—Speech, June 3, 1975

America's national pie is big enough for us all to share.

—Comments on farming policies, May 26, 1976

I hope for an America where the power of faith will always burn brightly, but where no modern inquisition of any kind will ever light the fires of fear, coercion, or angry division.

I hope for an America where we can all contend freely and vigorously, but where we will treasure and guard those standards of civility which alone make this nation safe for both democracy and diversity.

—Speech at Liberty University, October 3, 1983

Vital U.S. interests would clearly be served by implementing a lasting peace in Bosnia. All of us are familiar with the massacres and the atrocities that have characterized this brutal war. . . . Ending the carnage and restoring peace and stability to this part of Europe will prevent the kind of wider war that would inevitably involve the United States—and under far greater risk. Twice in this century Americans have died in battle in massive wars in Europe. . . . The peace, security, and freedom of Europe are still a vital interest of the United States today.

—Statement at Senate Armed Services hearing on Bosnia, November 18, 1995

Apartheid concerns everyone directly because it involves the whole future pattern of human relations. Apartheid is in conflict with the accepted principle of equality in rights of all human beings, and therefore it represents a challenge to the conscience of all mankind.

—Address, Senate Finance Committee, June 21, 1971

Will America support peoples of Africa who seek only the "unalienable rights" we sought and won ourselves two centuries ago? Or will we continue to follow policies that isolate us from these peoples—policies that place us on the side of minority governments that deny basic human rights, and that invite the involvement of other outside powers?

—*Speech, March 23, 1976*

ECONOMIC JUSTICE AND THE AMERICAN WORKER

TED KENNEDY WAS BORN INTO A RICH FAMILY; HE NEVER wanted for any material thing at any time in his life. Yet the whole of his adult career was a quest for economic justice. In every political fight over wages, tax equity, allocation of national resources, regulation of business and industry, he came down on the side of working families and the disadvantaged.

What explains this dedication to a purpose that so conflicts with his own economic interests? His editor and publisher, Jonathan Karp, interviewed by Terry Gross on NPR's "Fresh Air" program, suggested that his motivation sprang from two powerful influences, both from the very start of his life: First, his parents, Joseph and Rose Kennedy, though they ultimately "made it" in society, never stopped identifying with the struggles of the poor Irish immigrants from whom both were descended. They imparted to all their children a strong message not to forget their roots, and not to forget those still struggling, those subject to present-day discrimination and unequal access to the American dream. The second, equally powerful influence—perhaps surprising to those who think of Senator Kennedy as strong advocate for the "wall of separation between church and state"—was his Roman Catholic faith. He especially took to heart the verses in Matthew in which Jesus says that whoever serves the poor serves Him.

He translated that passion for service into effective legislative action, as President Barack Obama noted after his death: "For five decades, virtually every major piece of legislation to advance the civil rights, health and economic well being of the American people bore his name and resulted from his efforts."

It won't be "mission accomplished" on the economy until average Americans are secure in their jobs and can provide for their families.
—*As quoted in Reuters article, "Bush, advisers paint rosy picture of U.S. economy," August 9, 2005*

The history of our nation rests on the skills of its workers no less than on the achievements of its scholars.

—*Speech, October 19, 1975*

It's time to raise the minimum wage for America's lowest paid workers. This Sense of the Senate resolution can send a clear message that help is on the way for the lowest paid, hard-working Americans struggling to keep their families afloat and their dignity intact. It's wrong when a paycheck for a 40-hour work week isn't enough to feed a family of four. We intend to right that wrong by raising the minimum wage. We are talking about . . . real people. They are teacher's aides and child care workers. They work in clothing stores and airports. They clean and maintain buildings all across the country. . . . Their ability to support their families depends on whether we vote to increase the minimum wage.

—*Statement in support of the Sense of the Senate Resolution to Raise the Minimum Wage, March 25, 1999*

Americans are working harder and earning less. . . .
They are worried about losing their jobs, losing
their health insurance, affording their children's
education, caring for their elderly parents, and
somehow saving for their own retirement. The
rich are still getting richer, but more and more
families are left out and left behind. The rising
tide that once lifted all boats now lifts only the
yachts.

—*Statement on the introduction of*
The American Workers Economic Security Act,
quoted in Roll Call, March 25, 1996

Fewer hungry people are not good enough—we
want no hungry people anywhere in America.
It's a matter of simple justice.

—*End Hunger Now Rally,*
February 29, 2000

The Republican Congress raised their own pay
by a juicy $4,600 last year—but they continue
to block a fair raise for the nation's lowest paid
workers. Republican Members of Congress didn't
blink at giving themselves a pay raise. Yet they

deny—and continue to deny—a fair increase for workers at the bottom of the economic ladder. Our Republican friends preach the value of work—and then deny a fair day's pay for a full day's work.

—*White House Rally for the Minimum Wage,*
March 8, 2000

It is disgraceful that hard-working women and people of color are still battling wage disparities and pay discrimination on the job. There is a wealth of evidence that shows that the wage gap still continues to plague American families, and that wage discrimination continues to be a serious and pervasive problem in workplaces across the country. In spite of the progress we have made, women still earn only 76 cents for every dollar earned by men. African American women earn just 64 cents, and Latinas earn only 54 cents for every dollar earned by white men.

—*Statement on Equal Pay Day,*
April 3, 2001

These facts don't lie. Over the past three decades, the extraordinary benefits of our record prosperity have been flagrantly skewed in favor of the wealthiest members of society. Today, the top one percent of households have more wealth than the entire bottom 95 percent combined.

This extreme and widening disparity is disturbing, especially when so many Americans are working harder and longer. Parents are spending less and less time with their families—22 hours less a week, according to a study last year by the Council of Economic Advisers. Thirteen percent of all Americans are working a second job just to make ends meet. And these extra hours at work mean that the parents have less time to be with their children.

—*White House Rally for the Minimum Wage,*
March 8, 2000

A sound economy is the greatest social program America has ever had, the source of our hopes for action on all the other issues facing us.

—*Speech, April 2, 1976*

America cannot successfully compete with newly industrializing nations on the basis of which country can pay the lowest wages. It's a mistake to even try. It makes no sense to run a race to the bottom.

—Speech at the Conference of The National Association of Private Industry Councils, February 27, 1995

The American economy has deteriorated for more than two years, and the patient's vital signs continue to falter. President Bush and Republicans in Congress have responded by prescribing quack medicine—tax cuts for the wealthy that do nothing to cure the patient's illness. Even though the patient keeps getting worse, the President just keeps prescribing larger and larger doses of the same quack medicine, with a louder quack.

—Statement on the economy and the plight of America's workers, May 7, 2003

The aim of tax reform is not to plow up the whole garden but to get rid of the weeds so that we can let the flowers grow.

—Speech, July 1, 1977

People want to end loopholes in the tax laws, so that those who eat at the most expensive restaurants will pay their bill themselves, instead of making the Treasury foot the bill through tax deductions that are nothing more than food stamps for the rich.

—Speech, September 30, 1978

This issue [pension plan fairness] presents a stark choice about who we represent here in the Senate. "Which side are you on?" Are we on the side of the workers and retirees who struggle to find some economic security in their old age, or the side of the wheeler-dealers, corporate raiders, and the super-rich?

—Statement on pension plan reversions,
November 11, 1995

The sad fact is that today small companies and private citizens are Davids without slingshots, competing against corporate Goliaths in wars of attrition which have become increasingly difficult to win. The American people are not just concerned about "big government"—they are also concerned about the control exerted by "big business."

—*Speech, August 7, 1978*

Nearly one in five U.S. families is headed by a single woman—yet these women continue to earn the lowest average rate of pay. Women are entitled to the same paychecks as their male colleagues who are performing the same or comparable work. Without pay equality, women are less able to provide an economic safety net for themselves and their families.

—*Statement on Equal Pay Day,*
April 3, 2001

I regard competition as the cornerstone of our free enterprise system. Along with the Bill of Rights, it is the most important and distinguishing feature of our nation in the world community, a beacon for many other nations who are striving to emulate our two-hundred-year-old example of freedom and prosperity.

—Speech, June 30, 1977

For decades the labor movement has stood as a bulwark for freedom and democracy against tyranny around the world. The labor movement was essential in making America a strong society. Its advocacy of progressive legislation has brought immense benefits to all Americans, whether or not they have a union card.

—Statement on the North American Free Trade Agreement, November 20, 1993

HEALTH CARE:
SENATOR KENNEDY'S
LAST GREAT CHALLENGE

FINDING A WAY TO PROVIDE ALL AMERICANS WITH ACCESS to high quality health care has been something Ted Kennedy advocated from his very first term in the U.S. Senate in 1962. As the years went by and each proposal to accomplish the goal met with defeat, his determination increased. But the cause was still one among many; it did not become the central crusade of his life until 1973, when his twelve-year-old son Teddy, Jr. was stricken with cancer.

All at once he was plunged into a world of life-or-death medical decisions, grueling treatment schedules, and countless hours spent in waiting rooms with other parents of young cancer patients. He was there as a parent, not a politician, but the sounds and scenes in those waiting rooms stayed with him as no fact-finding tour or hearings on the state of health care could ever have done. Teddy, Jr. was fortunate to be admitted into an experimental treatment program that was highly promising for children with his form of cancer—at a cost of three thousand dollars per treatment. Three times per week for two years. While the protocol was still in the clinical trial phase, the government paid the bill; however, once the treatment was proven effective, the families were made to pick up the costs. In most cases their private insurance companies simply refused to pay.

So he saw many of these parents, who by this time he had come to know quite well, taking out second mortgages, or even forced to sell their homes. Some lost their jobs—and their health insurance—due to the time spent shuttling a sick child back and forth to the hospital for treatment. Bankruptcy and financial ruin loomed for people just like him, parents willing to do anything to save a child's life, but unlike him in their middle-class resources. From that point on, "the battle [for health care] had my complete attention."

And that is the way it remained to the last day of his life.

While I will not see the victory, I was able to look forward and know that we will—yes, we will—fulfill the promise of health care in America as a right and not a privilege.

> —*Letter to President Obama, May 12, 2009*

What we face is, above all, a moral issue; that at stake are not just the details of policy, but fundamental principles of social justice and the character of our country.

> —*Letter to President Obama, May 12, 2009.*
> *These were the lines directly quoted by*
> *the President in his address to the nation*
> *on health care reform, September 10, 2009*

For me this is a season of hope, new hope for a justice and fair prosperity for the many, and not just for the few—new hope. And this is the cause of my life—new hope that we will break the old gridlock and guarantee that every American—North, South, East, West, young, old—will have decent, quality health care as a fundamental right and not a privilege.

> —*Democratic National Convention,*
> *August 12, 1980*

Thirty-one years ago this summer, Dr. Martin Luther King led the March on Washington to demand basic human rights for all Americans. Today we have the chance to fulfill another part of that dream, by making health care a basic right.

—*Statement on health care reform, July 28, 1994*

If we deny the finest health care to any citizens, we deny the value of their lives. They become slaves of unnecessary suffering and disability. The promise of a beautiful society acquires a hollow ring. The American dream becomes a nightmare.

—*Speech, October 5, 1975*

What we have today in the United States is not so much a health-care system as a disease-care system.

—*Remarks on health care, May 31, 1994*

America doesn't need a double standard on health care: one for those who can afford it and another for those who can't.

—*Speech, February 1, 1976*

A world that is spending $300 billion a year for arms can spend a little more for health. And it may well be that what we do in health will be as important to world peace and cooperation in the long run as what we achieve in arms control, and at a tiny fraction of the cost.

—*Speech, May 6, 1977*

Too many elderly Americans today must choose between food on the table and the medicine they need to stay healthy or to treat their illnesses. Too many seniors take half the pills their doctor prescribes, or don't even fill needed prescriptions—because they cannot afford the high cost of prescription drugs. Too many seniors are paying twice as much as they should for the drugs they need, because they are forced to pay full price, while almost everyone with a private insurance policy benefits from negotiated discounts. Too many seniors are ending up hospitalized—at immense costs to Medicare—because they aren't receiving the drugs they need at all, or can't afford to take them correctly. Pharmaceutical products are increasingly the source of miracle cures for a host of dread diseases, but senior citizens are being left out and left behind because Congress fails to act.

—Statement at Senate Finance Committee
Hearings on Prescription Drug Coverage
for Seniors, March 29, 2000

Medicare is a specific contract between the people and their government. It says, "Work hard, pay into the trust fund during your working years, and you will have health security in your retirement years." Today's elderly kept their part of the bargain. They fought in World War II and Korea. They got up every morning, went to work, played by the rules, raised their families. Their hard work laid the foundation for the prosperity our country enjoys today. But our country's promise to them is being broken today and every day, because Medicare does not cover prescription drugs . . . . It is time to honor that promise.

—Statement at Senate Finance Committee
Hearings on Prescription Drug Coverage
for Seniors, March 29, 2000

Medicare and Social Security are two of the most successful programs ever enacted. They are a solemn commitment to all Americans—North, South, East, and West—that if they contribute to trust funds during their working years, they will have financial security and health security in their golden years.

—Speech on the 30th Anniversary of Medicare,
July 25, 1995

In any given year, one-third of the uninsured go without needed medical care. Eight million uninsured Americans fail to take medication their doctors prescribe because they cannot afford to fill the prescription. Four hundred thousand children suffering from asthma never see a doctor. Five hundred thousand children with recurrent earaches never see a doctor. Thirty-two thousand Americans with heart disease go without life-saving and life-enhancing bypass surgery or angioplasty— because they are uninsured. Twenty-seven thousand uninsured women are diagnosed with breast cancer each year. They are twice as likely as insured women not to receive medical treatment until their cancer has already spread in their bodies.

The chilling bottom line is that eighty-three thousand Americans die every year because they have no insurance. Being uninsured is the seventh leading cause of death in America. Our failure to provide health insurance for every citizen kills more people than kidney disease, liver disease, and AIDS combined.

—Statement on "President Bush's Fantasy Budget," February 21, 2001

Nurses are the backbone of an effective health care system. We cannot have a quality health care system without quality care by nurses.

—Statement urging the passage of the Nurse Reinvestment Act, July 22, 2002

With the sole exception of South Africa, no other industrialized nation in the world leaves its citizens in fear of financial ruin because of illness.

—Senate speech, December 9, 1978

As the crisis continues, it becomes more and more difficult for anyone to pretend that AIDS is someone else's problem. There are few of us who do not know someone who is either infected or affected by AIDS. In a very real way, we are all living with AIDS.

—*Statement, May 14, 1996*

One of our greatest fears as human beings is that one day we'll learn that we—or a loved one—have cancer, Alzheimer's, diabetes, Parkinson's, or any of a number of dread and deadly diseases. But every day, thousands of Americans are stunned by that bad news. The phone rings. The doctor is on the line. And lives are changed forever by the awful news.

Stem cell research holds the greatest promise of hope for the millions of Americans who face these diseases. Research on these tiny cells may mean that the next time a doctor gives the bad news of horrible disease, the doctor can also say that these diseases are now curable.

—*Statement at hearing on stem cell research, September 5, 2001*

Access to mental health services is one of the most important civil rights issues facing the nation. For too long, persons living with mental disorders have suffered discriminatory treatment at all levels of society. They have been forced to pay more for the services they need and to worry about their job security if their employer finds out about their condition. Sadly, in America today, patients with biochemical problems in their liver are treated with more compassion than those with biochemical problems in their brain. That kind of discriminatory treatment must end. No one questions the need for affordable treatment of physical illnesses. But those who suffer from mental illnesses face serious barriers in obtaining the services they need at prices they can afford. Like those suffering from physical illnesses, persons with mental disorders deserve quality care. Failure to obtain treatment can mean years of shattered dreams and unfulfilled potential. Americans with mental illness deserve health and happiness too—just as do those with physical illness.

—*Remarks on the Mental Health Equitable Treatment Act, November 29, 2001*

When I thought of all the years, all the battles, and all the memories of my long public life, I felt confident in these closing days that while I will not be there when it happens, you [President Obama] will be the President who at long last signs into law the health care reform that is the great unfinished business of our society. For me, this cause stretched across decades; it has been disappointed, but never finally defeated. It was the cause of my life. And in the past year, the prospect of victory sustained me—and the work of achieving it summoned my energy and determination.

—*Letter to President Obama, May 12, 2009*

IN LIGHTER MOMENTS

Ted Kennedy loved to laugh. So many of the speakers who paid him tribute at his memorial service recalled times spent with him, laughing. That hearty, booming, generous laugh that his friends so loved to hear. He loved a good joke or funny story, and of course, like any good Irish politician, he could spin a fine yarn. His humor was never mean-spirited; he was often self-deprecating, always quick to laugh at his own foibles and quirks.

Of course, he found it easy enough to poke fun at the Republicans, too: They gave him plenty of good shots. Many of us remember how he used the opportunity at his speech at the Democratic National Convention of 1988. Then-Vice President George Bush was the Republican nominee. Reagan was finishing up his second term, leaving office as the public was still wondering who did what in the Iran-Contra arms-trading deal. Bush claimed not to have known what was going on. "Where was George?" Kennedy asked the thousands of assembled delegates. He came up with more examples of the Vice President's absence while scandals were breaking out in the Reagan administration, one after the other. "Where was George?" Kennedy asked again, and this time the crowd chanted along with him. Then he was on a roll: He'd name a Reagan era policy mess, and the crowd would roar, "Where was George?" He had the rhythm down pat and the crowd chanting, clapping, and laughing along with him.

While the mood was light and the crowd played along, behind the laughter there was a question worth thinking about. Why *wasn't* the Vice President involved in each of the policy matters that affected so many millions of Americans? While Kennedy made his point with humor, at the core of the question was a concern that still resonated after the laughter was gone.

That was often the case with even his lightest remarks: that you knew he cared. When he heard that North Carolina Senator (and arch-conservative) Jesse Helms, scheduled to undergo heart surgery, had quipped beforehand, "It's no piece of cake, but it sure beats listening to Ted Kennedy on the Senate floor," he sent him this get-well note: "I would be happy to send you tapes of my recent Senate speeches if that will help your speedy recovery."

If, as the old saw has it, laughter is the best medicine, then Ted Kennedy was a wonderfully skilled healer.

We have learned that it is important to take issues seriously, but never to take ourselves too seriously.

—Speech at Harvard, December 2008

Well, here I *don't* go again.

—Remark on announcing that he is not running for president in 1988

Finally, after all of these years, when someone says, "Who does that damn Kennedy think he is," there's only a one in three chance they're talking about me.

—Remark following the election of his son Patrick to Congress, joining nephew Joseph Kennedy II.

Frankly, I don't mind not being president. I just mind that someone else is.

—Speech at the Washington Gridiron Club dinner,
March 1986

They [the Moral Majority] seem to think it's easier for a camel to pass through the eye of a needle than for a Kennedy to come to the campus of Liberty Baptist College.

—Speech at Liberty Baptist College,
October 3, 1983

She's a wonderful, wonderful person, and we're looking to a happy and wonderful night . . . er, life.

—Comment about Victoria Reggie,
to whom he had just become engaged

Well, I learned to lose, and for a Kennedy, that's hard.

—Answer to the question of what he'd learned from
his failed run for the Democratic nomination
for President in 1980

It's a privilege to be here tonight among friends. It isn't always that way. Not long ago, I was addressing a group, and shortly after I started speaking, a heckler in the audience jumped to his feet and shouted: "Senator Kennedy is a horse's rear end." I'm paraphrasing slightly. Right away, members of the audience rushed to my defense. They threw the heckler out, and told him never to come back. So I said to the chairman of the event, "I had no idea this was Kennedy country." And the chairman said, "It isn't. It's horse country."

—*Remarks at the American Constitution Society Conference, September 25, 2002*

It's a frequent joke in Democratic circles, as you may have heard, that for Republicans, life begins at conception and ends at birth. We know it's not true, and it's certainly not true for education.

—*Commencement address at Springfield College, May 14, 2006*

On hearing that Arnold Schwarzenegger, the husband of his niece Marie Shriver, and a lone Republican in a family of Democrats, was going to run for governor of California:

He's a brilliant actor, but what makes Republicans think he could do well in politics? Of course, it's hard to argue with Arnold when you're hanging upside down by the ankles.

—2003

Though very near the end of his life himself, Ted Kennedy found time to call Senator Chris Dodd, who was recuperating from prostate surgery. Kennedy told him:

Well, between going through prostate cancer surgery and going to town hall meetings [on the Obama health care plan], you made a great choice!

—Recounted by Senator Dodd at the memorial service for Ted Kennedy, August 28, 2009

Speak of a vision, work hard, and get a good road map of Iowa.

—*Quip when asked his advice for candidates for president, as quoted in* Newsweek, *July 13, 1987*

Upon hearing his father, Joseph Kennedy, Sr., the newly appointed U.S. Ambassador to Great Britain, repeatedly addressed as "Your Excellency," then-six-year-old Teddy Kennedy asked:

"Is that your new name, Daddy?"

—*As reported in* The Daily Mail, *March 17, 1938*

PERSONAL REFLECTIONS

PERSONAL REFLECTIONS

Growing up Kennedy means growing up in an atmosphere of high achievement, expectation of public service, and unquestioning devotion to family, faith, and country. Both parents made these demands of their children, but the patriarch of the family, Joseph P. Kennedy, had another expectation that he made explicit: Kennedys do not complain. They never whine. "There's no crying in this house," he decreed.

All nine of his children were taught this lesson but those who survived to bring up their own families came to break away from this stoic creed. Suffering in silence, as many can testify, can be damaging to the soul. There's something to be said for finding ways to acknowledge the hurts

179

and losses of life and to reflect on the meaning of painful events, and then share those reflections with those whose love and understanding can be counted on. It's not weakness to seek out a trusted soul under these circumstance; on the contrary, it can be a great source of strength.

But that's not the way Ted Kennedy had been brought up to think, and so, as he suffered loss after loss—with each sibling's early death, with his son Teddy, Jr.'s battle with cancer, and throughout so many other tragedies and sorrows—he simply pushed himself on, working more, attending more events, and yes, drinking too much and partying too hard. His first marriage broke down as a result. It was not until he met the woman who would become his second wife—Victoria Reggie—that he found a way to get off that dangerous road. She introduced him to the value of looking honestly at oneself, of grappling with his own painful emotions. She opened him up to himself.

We are the beneficiaries of this change in his outlook, which enabled him to put down on paper so many beautiful and deeply moving thoughts that would otherwise be forever lost. The writings that came out of the final year of his life—particularly his posthumously published memoir, *True*

Compass—give us passages stunning in their depth of feeling, all the more so for the often lyrical and even haunting quality of the prose. In the end he reveals himself to be a writer of great insight into his own soul, and he should be remembered for that, as much as for any of his grand orations before entranced crowds.

Asked by the Jonathan Karp, the publisher of his 2009 memoir True Compass, *how he dealt with all the loss in his life, Senator Kennedy answered:*

I think the reason I have been so restless in my life is that I have been trying to stay ahead of the darkness, to just keep moving to stay ahead of the despair.

—*As quoted by Jonathan Karp in* The Washington Post, *September 13, 2009*

I recognize my own shortcomings—the faults in the conduct of my private life. I realize that I alone am responsible for them, and I am the one who must confront them. I believe that each of us as individuals must not only struggle to make a better world, but to make ourselves better, too.

—*Speech to his constituents,*
Oct. 25, 1991

Sailing on *Mya* [his boat] with Vicki at my side and my dogs, Splash and Sunny, at my feet. And, of course, a Democrat in the White House and regaining our majority in the Senate.

—*Response to May 2006* Vanity Fair *interview question, "What is your idea of perfect happiness?"*

I do not seek to escape responsibility for my actions by placing the blame either on the physical and emotional trauma brought on by the accident, or on anyone else. I regard as indefensible the fact that I did not report the accident to the police immediately.

—Public statement after the
Chappaquiddick accident,
July 25, 1969

That night on Chappaquiddick Island ended in a horrible tragedy that haunts me every day of my life. I had suffered sudden and violent loss far too many times, but this night was different. This night I was responsible. . . . Yes, it was an accident. But that doesn't erase the fact that I had caused an innocent woman's death.

Atonement is a process that never ends. I believe that. Maybe it's a New England thing, or an Irish thing, or a Catholic thing. Maybe all of those things. But it's as it should be.

—True Compass: A Memoir, *2009*

I'm not afraid to die.

> —*Said in response to a reporter's question soon after the assassination of his brother Robert in June, 1968*

You want power because it's an opportunity.

> —*Remark, 1980*

[T]he pursuit of the presidency is not my life. Public service is.

> —*From Senator Kennedy's declaration that he would not run for President in 1988*

To a person in public life, nothing is more distressing today than the massive cynicism, hostility, and outright distrust that is undermining the people's basic faith and confidence in government and its institutions.

> —*Speech, September 10, 1976*

One of my favorite Seuss classics is "Horton Hears A Who". . . . In that story, the Mayor of Who-ville involves everyone in his community to help save their small town. It is the smallest Who that saves the day and empowers young people with the knowledge that they can make a difference. It is a lesson that my mother taught all of her children. I was the youngest in my family so I always had a soft spot for that little Who that had a hard time finding his own voice.

—*Remarks at the dedication of the*
Dr. Seuss National Memorial
in Springfield, MA, Mar 31, 2002

In his memoir True Compass *Ted Kennedy wrote of how in the blur of days following the assassination of his brother Robert, he often found refuge in sailing.*

I surrendered myself to the sea and the wind and the sun and the stars on these voyages. I let my mind drift, when it would, from my sorrows to a semblance of the momentous joy I have always felt at the way a sailboat moves through the water. I love sailing in the day, but there's something special about sailing at night. And on these nights in particular, my grieving was subsumed into a sense of oneness with the sky and the sea. The darkness helped me feel the movement of the sea, and it helped displace the emptiness inside me with the awareness of *direction*. An awareness that there is a beginning to the voyage and an end to the voyage, and that this beginning and ending is a part of the natural order of things.

—True Compass, *2009*

As a young boy, I was taught to live by the words in the 25th chapter of St. Matthew's Gospel where the Lord said that when we care for the least of those among us—the hungry, the thirsty, the sick, and the destitute—we are also caring for Him.

—*Speech, March 14, 2005*

All of my life, the teachings of my faith have provided solace and hope, as have the wonders of nature, especially the sea, where religion and spirituality meet the physical. This faith has been as meaningful to me as breathing or loving my family. It's all intertwined.

—True Compass: A Memoir, *2009*

The greatest blessing to me of my more recent years has been my wife Vicki's presence in my life. . . . Our conversations are long, our banter is fast, and her humor keeps life fun. Words are very much a part of our lives, but it is also the quiet moments when, hand in hand, we invite the stillness in, which truly sustains my faith and touches my heart.

—True Compass: A Memoir, *2009*

From the letter that he wrote to Pope Benedict XVI, hand-delivered by President Obama:

I am writing with deep humility to ask that you pray for me as my own health declines. I was diagnosed with brain cancer more than a year ago and although I continue treatment, the disease is taking its toll on me. I am 77 years old and preparing for the next passage of life. I have been blessed to be part of a wonderful family and both of my parents, particularly my mother, kept our Catholic faith at the center of our lives. That gift of faith has sustained and nurtured and provides solace to me in the darkest hours. I know that I have been an imperfect human being, but with the help of my faith I have tried to right my path. I want you to know, Your Holiness, that in my nearly 50 years of elective office I have done my best to champion the rights of the poor and open doors of economic opportunity. I have worked to welcome the immigrant, to fight discrimination and expand access to health care and education. I have opposed the death penalty and fought to end war. Those are the issues that have motivated me and have been the focus of my work as a United States senator. I also want you to know that even though I am ill, I am committed to do everything I can to achieve access to health care for everyone in my country. This has been the political cause of my life. I believe in a conscience protection for Catholics in the health field and I will continue to advocate for it as my colleagues in the Senate and I work to develop an overall national health policy that guarantees health care for everyone. I have always tried to be a faithful Catholic, Your Holiness, and though I have fallen short through human failings, I have never failed to believe and respect the fundamental teachings of my faith. I continue to pray for God's blessings on you and on our church and would be most thankful for your prayers for me.

—July 2009

ACKNOWLEDGMENTS

We are grateful for the assistance of our senior researcher, John Peter Kaytrosh. Peggy Robin's insight and editorial judgment were invaluable in putting this book together. Claire Adler's fast fingers helped us get the book done on time. Jeanne Welsh was instrumental in bringing this book into being, and Karen Adler made a very helpful suggestion as we got started. We appreciate Claiborne Hancock's foresight and hard work in getting this book done so swiftly. Without the help of numerous people at Pegasus, this book would never have found its way into your hands, and we would especially like to thank Maria Fernandez for interior design, Michael Fusco whose talent you see as the book's cover, Phil Gaskill who noticed our typos and more, and Michael Levatino and Deirdre Dolan, who revealed to bookstores the wisdom of carrying *The Wit and Wisdom of Ted Kennedy.*